P9-AON-593

Education/Psychology Journals:
A Scholar's Guide

by

Darlene Baden Arnold

and

Kenneth O. Doyle, Jr.

The Scarecrow Press, Inc.
Metuchen, N.J.   1975

Library of Congress Cataloging in Publication Data

Arnold, Darlene Baden, 1948-
    Education/psychology journals.

    Includes index.
    1. Educational psychology--Periodicals. I. Doyle,
Kenneth O. , joint author. II. Title.
LB1051. A732   370. 15'05   74-23507
ISBN 0-8108-0779-3

TABLE OF CONTENTS

iii

124610

INTRODUCTION

This guide contains detailed descriptions of 122
journals of professional interest to many psychologists, educationists, educational psychologists, and educators. We in-
tend it to help these people decide which journals to read
and subscribe to and to which to submit their professional
manuscripts. Students in psychology and education, scholars
whose work embraces both these fields, and people for whom
budgets and professional obligations require efficient decisions about periodicals should find this guide particularly
helpful.

Defining our domain of interest was difficult indeed,
since there are thousands of journals that might have been
included. After much deliberation we settled on an admittedly
subjective procedure. From a list of journals searched both
by Psychological Abstracts and ERIC (Current Index to Journals in Education) we eliminated journals that we felt did not
publish with reasonable regularity articles bearing on the
interface of psychology and education. We excluded mental
health, counseling, and psychotherapy journals unless their
content often seemed relevant to this interface. We also
omitted journals that, in our opinion, would be of interest
primarily to very small and highly specialized professional
groups. We included journals whose primary focus is research methodology, so long as that methodology appeared
germane to educational/psychological research. Our final
selection, we believe, more than adequately covers the domain of periodicals that intersect psychology and education.

With the help of a number of colleagues, we developed
a list of questions, the answers to which would be important
for deciding to read or submit manuscripts to a journal.
We sent a questionnaire to the editor of each of the journals
described above. Whenever possible, we also examined a
recent number of the periodical.

More than 90 per cent of the editors responded. For the remaining journals, we supplied the descriptions from our own examination of the journals. If a description is exclusively ours, we note that fact in the List of Entries (following the Introduction) by an asterisk (*).

We condensed and edited the questionnaire responses, sent the responding editors copies of their journal's entries for prepublication review, and made revisions as necessary. We believe this process virtually assures the reliability of the information contained in this guide, but we make no warranty with regard to the accuracy of the entries. Readers are urged to consult recent issues of journals under consideration.

Entries are arranged alphabetically and numbered serially. The typical entry includes:

JOURNAL NAME (Year Founded) Subtitle

    Former Title

Editor and Editorial Address

Publisher and Copyright Holder

Subscription Data
    Subscription Cost
    Frequency of Issue
    Circulation
    Approximate Number of Pages per Issue (exclusive of advertising)

Typical Content Areas of Articles

Typical Disciplines and Professional Specialties of Readers and Contributors

Intended Audience

Special Features of Journal Content

Acceptance/Rejection Criteria (Summary of journal's criteria for accepting/rejecting manuscripts)

Acceptance/Rejection Procedures (Summary of journal's procedures for accepting/rejecting manuscripts)

Manuscript Disposition
    Receipt of manuscript acknowledged?
    Time required for editorial decision?

Author nominates referees?
"Blind" refereeing?
Critique to author?
Rejected manuscript returned?
Approximate percentage of submitted manuscripts accepted for publication (including conditionally accepted)
Approximate number of manuscripts published per year (excluding letters, notes)
Time required for accepted manuscript to be published
Are manuscripts published on a "first accepted, first published" basis?

Style Requirements
Statement of journal's style requirements
Preferred length of manuscript (also minimum, maximum lengths)
Number of copies submitted
Abstract required?

Payment or Page Charges

Reprints (availability, cost, etc.)

The completeness and length or brevity of an entry is directly related to the editor's questionnaire responses.

A bibliography of style manuals required or recommended by the various journals, a list of periodical indices and abstracts that reference these journals, and an extensive subject index are provided for convenience.

We thank all those who helped us, particularly Jerry King, the late Ralph Berdie, David P. Campbell, and Darwin D. Hendel for constructive and supportive comments during the early stage of the project; the editors of the journals, without whose cooperation this guide would not have been possible; and our spouses, who persevered.

LIST OF ENTRIES

*Annotated without benefit of review by editor of journal.

1 ACADEMIC THERAPY (1965)
formerly Academic Therapy Quarterly

John Arena, 1539 4th St., San Rafael, CA 94901
Publisher & Copyright: Academic Therapy Publications, Inc.
Above address
Subscriptions: Instit. & Indiv. $6/yr. Six issues a year,
four regular, and two newsletter editions. Ca. 8500.
128 pages/issue.

Description: "International, interdisciplinary quarterly for
professionals and parents who are concerned with the
identification, diagnosis, and remediation of intellectually
capable children who are academically underachieving."
Article Content: Visual and auditory perception; motor co-
ordination; speed of perception; perceptual discrimination; ocular tracking; learning disabilities; reading dys-
functions.
Intended Audience: Classroom & special teachers; researchers; practitioners; educational therapists; parents.
Special Features: Research reports; theoretical articles;
book reviews; letters to the editor; annual index; readers' reply and product services; available on microform; advertising.

Acceptance/Rejection Procedures: MSS pertinent to the field
are accepted if there is not a long waiting line of previously accepted MSS.
Manuscript Disposition: Receipt of MS acknowledged; 3 to
4 weeks required for decision; rejected MS returned
(include stamped, self-addressed envelope); 20% submitted MSS accepted; 60 MSS published/yr; 3 to 4
issues between acceptance/publication; first accepted,
first published.
Style Requirements: University of Chicago Press Manual of

Style; preferred length 10 pages, double spaced; no
minimum, 15 page maximum length (should have previous agreement to exceed 10, though); abstract not required; two copies of MS.
Payment: None to or by author for publication.
Reprints: 50 free; charge for additional depends on length of
article.

2 ALBERTA JOURNAL OF EDUCATIONAL RESEARCH (1955)

Dr. John McLeish, Faculty of Education, University of Alberta, Edmonton, Canada T6G 2E1
Publisher: Faculty of Education
Subscriptions: Instit. & Indiv. $6/yr. Quarterly. Ca. 750.
80 pages/issue.

Description: "Aims to publish quality articles dealing with
historical, philosophical, empirical research related to
the educational system and process. Comparative articles
are also welcomed."
Typical Disciplines: Psychology/education; administration
(educ.); foundations of educ.; elementary and secondary
education.
Intended Audience: Researchers; beginning graduate students
in education; advanced graduate students and specialists;
teachers; administrators; practitioners.
Special Features: Research reports; theoretical articles;
book reviews; abstract for each article; cumulative index
for period 1955-1965.

Acceptance/Rejection Criteria: In desired format; properly
researched; relevant to educational problems; constitutes
something new, insightful.
Acceptance/Rejection Procedures: Discussion & disposition
of MSS are the joint responsibility of the Publication
Committee. Referees' opinions may be called upon as
to suitability.
Manuscript Disposition: Receipt of MS acknowledged; 3
months required for decision; rejected MS returned;
50% submitted MSS accepted; 30 MSS published/yr.
3-6 months from acceptance to publication.
Style Requirements: APA Publication Manual and issue of
journal; preferred length 4000 words; 2000 word minimum, 6000 word maximum; 2 copies of MS required;
abstract of 100 words on separate page.
Payment: None to or by author for publication.

Reprints: 20 free; nominal charge for additional copies.

3   AMERICAN BEHAVIORAL SCIENTIST (1957)
     formerly Prod (name change 1960)

Publisher & Copyright: Sage Publications, Inc., 275 So.
     Beverly Drive, Beverly Hills, CA 90212 (Address all
     correspondence to this address)
Subscriptions: Instit. $24/yr. Indiv. $12/yr. Student
     (U.S. & Canada only) $9/yr. Bimonthly (since 1967).
     160 pages/issue.

Description: "Each issue is prepared under the direction of
     a guest editor, and focuses on a specific theme from
     the emerging areas of cross-disciplinary interest in the
     social sciences."
Article Content: Police and society; society and the aging;
     professions in contemporary society; people-processing
     institutions; mass communications and youth; world cities
     of the future; learning to work.
Typical Disciplines: All social scientists, including political
     scientists, psychologists, communication theorists.
Intended Audience: General and college-educated public;
     undergraduate and beginning graduate students in psy-
     chology; advanced graduate students and specialists;
     teachers; researchers; practitioners.
Special Features: Special theme each issue, with guest
     editor; incorporates New Studies, an extensive annotated
     bibliography covering important recent publications in the
     social and behavioral sciences; annual index; available
     on microform; advertising.

Acceptance/Rejection Criteria and Procedures: Guest editors
     are charged with full responsibility for soliciting MSS
     and quality control.
Manuscript Disposition: MSS solicited by editors; 50-60 MSS
     published/yr.
Style Requirements: Available upon request from guest editor
     or Sage; preferred length 15-30 pages, double spaced;
     no minimum, 40 page maximum length; 2 copies of MS;
     no abstract.
Payment: None to or by author for publication.
Reprints: 24 free; charge for additional depends on page
     length.

4   AMERICAN EDUCATION MAGAZINE (1965)
     formerly School Life

Leroy V. Goodman, U.S. Office of Education, 400 Maryland
    Ave. S.W., Washington, D.C.   20202
Publisher: U.S. Office of Education
Subscriptions: $9.95/yr. Issued 10 times yearly including
    Jan.-Feb. and August-Sept. Ca. 40,000. 36 pages/
    issue.

Description: "As the official journal of the U.S. Office of
    Education, serves to interpret and explain exemplary pro-
    grams being carried out with federal support. The maga-
    zine also reflects 'official' policies and viewpoints in
    articles prepared by Federal administrators. "
Article Content: Articles provide the reader with the specific
    information he would need to launch and carry out such
    a program himself--what is unusual about it, why it was
    organized, and how; what goals were established; what
    obstacles were overcome; what kinds of people and re-
    sources were necessary; how it operates; what those in-
    volved think about it; what evidence indicates the program
    is working.
Typical Disciplines: School and college administrators.
Intended Audience: Teachers; researchers; administrators;
    practitioners; legislators; members of school boards; li-
    brarians; PTA members.
Special Features: Research reports; editorials; federal funds
    and educational statistic feature; recent publications on
    education and related areas prepared by the Federal gov-
    ernment; yearly guide to Office of Education-administered
    programs; annual index.

Acceptance/Rejection Criteria: Stories must deal with educa-
    tion programs or activities supported by federal funds.
    Writing should be bright and provocative, with emphasis
    on personalization and human interest. The stories must
    be free of jargon, and should serve a serious purpose--
    the education of educators and others directly concerned
    with education.
Manuscript Disposition: One week required for decision; no-
    tification of author by mail; rejected MS returned; 5%
    submitted MSS accepted; 50 MSS published/yr.; three
    months from acceptance to publication.
Style Requirements: Statement provided upon request; pre-
    ferred length 2500 words; minimum 1500 words, maximum
    5000; one copy of MS required; no abstract.

Payment: Authors paid for published MS; $225 and up depend-
ing on ability and reliability; guarantees from $100 to
$150.
Reprints: Only occasionally available; consult Editor.

5 AMERICAN EDUCATIONAL RESEARCH JOURNAL

Kaoru Yamamoto, College of Education, Arizona State Univer-
sity, Tempe, AZ 85281
Publisher and Copyright: American Educational Research
Association, 1126 Sixteenth Street, N.W., Washington,
D.C. 20036
Subscriptions: Inst. & Indiv. $10/yr. Free to members of
AERA. Quarterly.

Description: "Purpose is to carry original reports of empirical and theoretical studies in education."
Article Content: The AERA has eight divisions: administration, curriculum and objectives, instruction and learning,
measurement and research methodology, counseling and
human development, history and historiography, social
context of education, and school evaluation and program
development. Editorial discretion is exercised to balance
the character of the journal to reflect the full range and
variety of activities of AERA members. Attempt also
being made to broaden the perspective of educational research from the United States to the whole world.
Special Features: Research reports; theoretical articles;
brief notes; book reviews; editorials; abstract for each
article.

Acceptance/Rejection Procedures: Relies on a large number
of consultants selected from the general AERA membership and, if necessary, from outside the organization;
initial screening takes place according to the stated editorial stance; those MSS which seem to satisfy the needs
of the journal are sent to at least two of these consultants, selected on the basis of their particular areas of
competence, who are requested to examine it and arrive
at recommendations for its disposition.
Manuscript Disposition: 2 to 4 months, sometimes longer,
required for decision; "blind" refereeing; one of copies
of MS not returned under any circumstances; 6 months to
1 year from acceptance to publication.
Style Requirements: APA Publication Manual and journal; preferred length 5 to 15 pages; all copy double spaced;

original and two copies of MS; author's name and affiliation should appear on a separate cover page,' and only on
this page, to insure anonymity in reviewing; include, also
on separate pages, an abstract of 100-120 words, and a
biographical resume of the author and all coauthors, giving name, position, office address, degrees and institutions, areas of specialization, and AERA divisional membership.

Reprints: Copies may be ordered when galley proofs are
returned.

6 AMERICAN JOURNAL OF PSYCHOANALYSIS (1941)

Helen A. DeRosis, M.D., 329 East 62nd St., New York, NY
10021
Publisher & Copyright: Association for the Advancement of
Psychoanalysis, 329 East 62nd St., New York, NY 10021
Subscriptions: Instit. $22/yr. Indiv. $12/yr. Four times/
yr. beginning in 1974. Ca. 1500.

Description: "To communicate modern concepts of psychoanalytic theory and practice and related investigations in
allied fields. Fosters exchange of information and of dif-
fering theoretical points of view."
Article Content: Theoretical, clinical, and descriptive.
Typical Disciplines: Psychoanalysis; psychiatry; psychology;
social work; education; mental health.
Intended Audience: Beginning graduate students in psychology;
advanced graduate students & specialists; researchers;
practitioners.
Special Features: Research reports; theoretical articles;
book reviews; letters to the editor; editorials; hortatory
or polemical articles; brief communication; clinical ex-
cerpts; annual, cumulative index; advertising; extensive
expansion in 1974.

Acceptance/Rejection Criteria: Must be well prepared; in
field covered; of interest to the readership; journal provides opportunity for and encourages young workers.
Acceptance/Rejection Procedures: All pertinent MSS are submitted to Editorial Board (5 members) who accept out-
right, accept with reservations, return to author for
changes, reject. Inexperienced workers with a good subject are worked with on organization, clarification, elab-
oration of material.
Manuscript Disposition: Receipt of MS acknowledged; rejected

MS returned; critique to author; first accepted, first published.
Style Requirements: Consult journal; bibliography should follow Index Medicus style; preferred length 15-20 pages;
brief communications may be 2-3 pages; page policy generally flexible; 3 copies of MS required; abstract required,
on separate sheet, in triplicate.
Payment: None to author; charge will be made for excessive
galley changes.
Reprints: Available as requested; price varies.
Special Note: Most statistical data have been omitted since
this journal is undergoing expansion.

7 THE AMERICAN JOURNAL OF PSYCHOLOGY (1887)

Lloyd G. Humphreys, Psychology Building, University of
Illinois at Urbana-Champaign, Champaign, IL 61820
Publisher: University of Illinois Press, Urbana, IL 61801
Copyright: Board of Trustees of the University of Illinois
Subscriptions: Instit. & Indiv. $15/yr. Quarterly. Ca.
3000. 224 pages/issue.

Description: "Publishes articles or original research in general experimental psychology. Great breadth of coverage. "
Typical Disciplines: Experimental psychology and closely related disciplines in both the physical and social science
sides of psychology.
Intended Audience: Advanced graduate students & specialists.
Special Features: Research reports; book reviews; abstract
for each article; short notes and discussions; advertising.

Acceptance/Rejection Criteria: Subject matter must be experimental; problem must not be trivial; data clearly and
correctly analyzed; text well written; clarity of presentation a main objective; favors inclusion of well-designed
tables and figures. The ideal article describes the theoretical point of view that led to the research, evaluates
critically the most relevant research done on the topic,
and presents the results of the experiments in a replicable
way.
Acceptance/Rejection Procedures: Any one of 4 principal
editors can accept or reject an article; each utilizes consultants as needed.
Manuscript Disposition: Receipt of MS acknowledged; 60 days
required for decision; rejected MS returned; critique to

author; 33% submitted MSS accepted; 60-80 MSS published/ yr.; 9-12 months from acceptance to publication (lag decreasing substantially); first accepted, first published.
Style Requirements: APA Publication Manual; no page length requirements; 2 copies of MS; abstract required.
Payment: None to or by author for publication.
Reprints: Available (approximate cost $2 per page of article for 200 reprints).

8 AMERICAN PSYCHOLOGIST (1946)

Kenneth B. Little, American Psychological Association, 1200 17th Street N.W., Washington, D.C. 20036
Publisher & Copyright: American Psychological Association.
Subscriptions: Inst. & Indiv. $12/yr. Available on January through December basis only. Monthly. Ca. 37, 000. 96 pages/issue.

Description: "Is the official publication of the APA, publishing the official papers of the Association, archival documents, and substantive articles of psychology. Has a broad scope."
Article Content: Timely, of broad general interest to psychologists of all scientific and professional persuasions.
Intended Audience: Psychologists in general.
Special Features: April issue contains the highlights of the annual convention to be held the following September, and the December issue contains a list of all the papers presented at the convention; available on microform; annual index; advertising.

Acceptance/Rejection Procedures: MSS are sent to Associate Editors (in house) for review. They may be and usually are sent to outside reviewers. On the basis of the reviews of the Associate Editors and any outside reviews, the MS is accepted or rejected.
Manuscript Disposition: Receipt of MS acknowledged; 8-10 weeks required for decision; "blind" refereeing; rejected MS returned; critique to author; 37% submitted MSS accepted; 242 MSS published/yr. (including official publications); 6-8 months from acceptance to publication; first accepted, first published.
Payment: None to author; author may be charged for alterations on galley proofs.
Reprints: Available at charge from publisher.

9 THE AMERICAN SCHOLAR (1932)

Peter Gay, The American Scholar, 1811 Q Street, N.W.,
Washington, D.C. 20009
Publisher & Copyright: United Chapters of Phi Beta Kappa,
1811 Q Street N.W., Washington, D.C.
Subscriptions: Instit. & Indiv. $6.50/yr. Quarterly. Ca.
45,000. 176 pages/issue.

Description: "The Scholar is a general quarterly intended for
the intelligent layman, presenting nontechnical articles on
a variety of subjects."
Article Content: The arts, sciences, religion, politics, literature, current affairs, national and foreign affairs.
Intended Audience: General public.
Special Features: Book reviews; letters to the editor; literature reviews; annual index; advertising.

Acceptance/Rejection Criteria: Journal's intent is to have
articles by scholars and experts but written in nontechnical language for an intelligent audience. Material accepted covers a wide range of subject matter.
Acceptance/Rejection Procedures: To be accepted for publication a MS must receive the affirmative votes of the editor and at least 2 members of the editorial board.
Manuscript Disposition: Receipt of MS acknowledged; 2-3
weeks required for decision; "blind" refereeing; rejected
MS returned; 49 MSS (plus 4 to 6 short book reviews and
various poems) published/yr.; 3 to 6 months from acceptance to publication.
Style Requirements: Guide available from editor; minimum
length of MS 3500 words, maximum length 4000; 1 copy
of MS; abstract not required.
Payment: None by author; authors paid approximately $150
for published MSS.
Reprints: 3 copies of issue in which MS appears available
without charge; reprints may be ordered in 100s, priced
according to article length.

10 ANIMAL LEARNING & BEHAVIOR (1973)
formerly a part of Psychonomic Science

Abram Amsel, Department of Psychology, University of Texas,
Austin, TX 78712
Publisher & Copyright: The Psychonomic Society, Inc., 1018
W. 34th St., Austin TX 78705

Subscriptions: Instit. $12.50/yr. Indiv. $6.25/yr. Information from Publications Office, Psychonomic Society. Quarterly. 80 pages/issue.

Description: "To publish experimental, theoretical, and review articles and critical comments in the areas described by the title. To increase communications among those who share an interest in the learning and behavior of nonhuman, as well as human, animals."

Article Content: Conditioning and learning; motivation; developmental processes; social and sexual behavior; comparative investigations; sensory processes.

Typical Disciplines: Operant, classical conditioning; learning theory; comparative psychology; ethology; animal behavior; developmental behavior.

Intended Audience: Beginning graduate students in psychology; advanced graduate students; teachers; researchers; people in animal behavior who may be zoologists, ethologists, etc.

Special Features: Research reports; theoretical articles; critical reviews with a theoretical content (whose major impact is not bibliographic); abstract for each article; editorials; annual index.

Acceptance/Rejection Criteria: Criteria extremely high; experimental articles which report results of comprehensive investigations favored; theoretical articles should provide interesting and reasonable alternatives to existing ideas and reflect a familiarity with existing work; reviews should be critical, and not primarily bibliographic; this is not a highly specialized journal, so jargon should be kept to a minimum.

Acceptance/Rejection Procedures: Articles are acted on by the editor or an associate editor after usually two independent reviews by experts chosen for each particular article.

Manuscript Disposition: Receipt of MS acknowledged; 4-6 weeks required for decision; rejected MS returned; critique to author; 20-25% submitted MSS accepted; 80 MSS published/yr.; first accepted, first published.

Style Requirements: APA Publication Manual, also see journal, editorial office; no page length requirements within reasonable limits; 3 copies of MS; abstract required on separate page.

Payment: None to or by author.

Reprints: Available from editorial office.

11 BEHAVIOR THERAPY (1970)

Cyril M. Franks, The Psychological Clinic, Rutgers University, New Brunswick, NJ 08903
Publisher: Academic Press, 111 5th Ave., N.Y. 10003
Journal Affiliation: Association for Advancement of Behavior Therapy
Subscriptions: Instit. $40/yr. Indiv. non-member $16/yr. Indiv. member and students $11/yr. Issued 5/yr. Ca. 2000. 160 pages/issue.

Description: "An interdisciplinary journal primarily for the publication of the results of original research of an experimental or clinical nature which contributes to the theory or practice of behavior therapy or behavior modification in any setting."
Typical Disciplines: Clinical psychology; experimental psychology; psychiatry; social work; special education; medicine; neurology.
Intended Audience: Undergraduate, beginning and advanced graduate students in psychology and education; teachers; researchers; practitioners.
Special Features: Research reports; theoretical articles; book reviews; letters to the editor; literature reviews; "news and notes" section; abstract for each article; annual index; advertising.

Acceptance/Rejection Criteria: In addition to original research, contributions that critically analyze and discuss important theoretical, social, or ethical issues raised by the theory or practice of behavior therapy are welcomed; articles which critically review particular problems in field occasionally published; brief descriptions of new apparatus or techniques, case studies of unusual significance, and systematic appraisal of special programs accepted from time to time.
Acceptance/Rejection Procedures: Virtually all MSS sent to at least two referees who may or may not be members of the editorial board; editor or associate editor makes final decision.
Manuscript Disposition: Receipt of MS acknowledged; 6-8 weeks required for decision; rejected MS returned; detailed critique to author; 10% submitted MSS accepted; 80-90 MSS published/yr.; 6-12 months from acceptance to publication; first accepted, first published.
Style Requirements: APA Publication Manual and journal; preferred length 6-12 pages, double spaced; two copies

of MS; page 2 should contain short abstract of not more than 150 to 200 words.

Payment: None to or by author.

Reprints: 50 free; additional ordered with galley proof.

Special Note: In addition to Dr. Franks, MSS may be sent to the Associate Editor, John Paul Brady, M.D., Hospital of the University of Pennsylvania, 1141 Gates Buildings, Philadelphia, PA 19104

12 BRITISH JOURNAL OF EDUCATIONAL PSYCHOLOGY (1931)

Professor John Nisbet, Department of Education, University of Aberdeen, King's College, Aberdeen, Scotland.

Publisher: Scottish Academic Press, 25 Perth Street, Edinburgh, EH 3 5 DW

Journal Affiliation: British Psychological Society and ATCDE (Association of Teachers in Colleges and Departments of Education)

Subscriptions: Instit. & Indiv. $13.50/yr. 3 issues/year in Feb., June, and Nov. Ca. 4200. 360 pages/issue.

Description: "To report empirical research studies in the field of educational psychology. The major European journal (in English) in the field."

Article Content: Educational psychology; empirical studies of learning and teaching; personality; social psychology in an educational context; educational assessment.

Intended Audience: Advanced graduate students & specialists; educational psychologists; university teachers of educational psychology; researchers.

Special Features: Research reports; research and critical notes; book reviews; abstract for each article; advertising.

Acceptance/Rejection Criteria: Contribution to educational psychology, theoretical, practical, or methodological; sound empirical basis--good design, adequate sampling, appropriate measures, accurate analysis, valid conclusions; clarity of writing--economy in words, no technical jargon, readable style; timeliness of topic; research reports only.

Acceptance/Rejection Procedures: Screening by editorial board; comment from referees; decision by editor.

Manuscript Disposition: Receipt of MS acknowledged; one month required for decision; rejected MS returned; critique to author; 25% submitted MSS accepted; 45 MSS

published/yr.; 8 months from acceptance to publication;
first accepted, first published.
Style Requirements: See November issue of journal; preferred
length 3000 words; minimum 1000, maximum 4000 words;
2 copies of MS; abstract required.
Payment: None to or by authors.
Reprints: 50 free; cost for additional depends on article
length.

13 CALIFORNIA JOURNAL OF EDUCATIONAL RESEARCH
(1949)

William P. Osborn, San Jose State University, San Jose,
California 95192
Publisher & Copyright: California Teachers Association,
1705 Murchison Drive, Burlingame, CA 94010
Subscriptions: Indiv. $10/yr. Issued 5/yr. in Jan., March,
May, September, and November. Ca. 1000. 48 pages/
issue.

Description: "Contents of the journal include articles reporting original research in the field of education; critical
reviews of past research or seminars of research in progress in any important aspect of educational practice, reports of demonstration projects based on concepts devised
for research; covers all levels--elementary, secondary,
and college. "
Intended Audience: Beginning graduate students in psychology
and education; advanced graduate students & specialists;
researchers; administrators; practitioners; teachers.
Special Features: Research reports; theoretical articles;
book reviews; abstract for each issue; editorials; digests
of theses and dissertations; information about newly initiated or recently completed projects in California universities, colleges, and school districts; annual and cumulative index, available on microform.

Manuscript Disposition: Receipt of MS acknowledged; 3 months
required for decision; "blind" refereeing; MS returned if
author so requests and includes a stamped, self-addressed
envelope; 25% submitted MSS accepted; 25 MSS published/
yr.; one year from acceptance to publication; first accepted, first published.
Style Requirements: APA Publication Manual and see journal;
preferred length 1500 to 3000 words, not including tables;
double space, 2 copies of MS; tables, charts and graphs

clearly and accurately titled, inked to size, and placed within the text material at appropriate place in MS; abstract of not more than 150 words required.

Payment: None to or by author.

Reprints: 3 copies of Journal furnished; additional charge depends on article length.

14   CANADIAN AND INTERNATIONAL EDUCATION (1972)

Editorial Address: Canadian and International Education, Room S-829, Ontario Institute for Studies in Education, 252 Bloor St. W., Toronto, Ontario, Canada M5S IV6.

Publisher & Copyright: Comparative and International Education Society of Canada.

Subscriptions: Instit. & Indiv. $6/yr. Students $3/yr. Issued twice a year in June and December. 100 pages/issue.

Description: "Devoted to the publication of articles dealing with education and society in Canada and in other nations. Journal's interest is the continuing study of educational theories and practices as they develop and change in various societies. Journal's concern is the clarification of the role of education in promoting understanding and harmonious relationships within and between nations."

Article Content: Articles dealing with features, issues and problems of education in various local, provincial and regional areas in Canada; comparative studies of the distinctive and distinguishing features of the various educational systems in Canada; articles dealing with features, issues and problems of education in various nations; comparative studies of aspects of education in various parts of the world.

Typical Disciplines: Journal's policy is to include articles by writers who do not necessarily claim to be comparative educationists but who are concerned with the various social and environmental forces as they impinge on education in different societies.

Special Features: Book reviews; letters to the editor; abstracts of dissertations; special theme for some issues; MSS in either French or English; abstract for each article (100 words).

15   CANADIAN JOURNAL OF BEHAVIORAL SCIENCE (1969)

James Inglis, Department of Psychology, Queen's University,

Kingston, Ontario, Canada.
Journal Affiliation & Copyright: Canadian Psychological Association (CPA), 1390 Sherbrooke St. W., Montreal 109, Quebec.
Subscriptions: $20/yr. (from CPA, Business Office). Quarterly. Ca. 1200. 100 pages/issue.

Description: "To publish articles in the applied areas of psychology and both research and theoretical articles in the areas of social, personality, abnormal, education, developmental, and child psychology."
Article Content: Social, personality, clinical, educational, developmental, and industrial psychology.
Intended Audience: Advanced graduate students & specialists; teachers; researchers; practitioners.
Special Features: Research reports; theoretical articles; editorials; literature reviews; abstract for each article; annual index; advertising.

Acceptance/Rejection Criteria: MS should deal with areas relevant to journal's interest; papers on practical, clinical issues encouraged; brief case reports with theoretical or practical implications will be considered.
Acceptance/Rejection Procedures: MS reviewed by at least two peer consultants (often including a member of the Editorial Board); reviews then evaluated by the Editor and two Assistant Editors.
Manuscript Disposition: Receipt of MS acknowledged; 4 months required for decision; rejected MS returned; critique to author; 25-30% submitted MSS accepted; 40 MSS published/yr.; 12 months from acceptance to publication; first accepted, first published (usually).
Style Requirements: APA Publication Manual; preferred length 15 pages, double spaced; no minimum, 20 page maximum length; 3 copies of MS; abstract of up to 100 words required.
Payment: None to author; author may be charged if paper is much longer than usual.
Reprints: Charge depends on length.

16 CANADIAN JOURNAL OF PSYCHOLOGY

Dr. P. C. Dodwell, Department of Psychology, Queen's University, Kingston, Ontario, Canada.
Publisher: University of Toronto Press. Copyright: Canadian Psychological Association and University of Toronto Press.

Subscriptions: $20/yr. Available from the Canadian Psychological Association, Business Office, 1390 Sherbrooke Street West, Montreal 109, Quebec. Available on calendar-year basis only. Quarterly. Ca. 1000-2000. 118 pages/issue.

Description: "Publishes experimental and theoretical articles in all recognized fields of psychology."
Special Features: Research reports; theoretical articles; abstract for each article; annual index; advertising.

Acceptance/Rejection Criteria: Contributors need not be members of C. P. A. MSS may be in either French or English.
Style Requirements: Consult journal; maximum length 12 pages; double space throughout; 2 copies of MS; abstract of up to 100 words required; be sure that complete address is given and in the case of one or more authors, the name and address of the author to whom the proofs should be sent.
Payment: Author charged approximately $60/printed page for an article exceeding 12 printed pages; in the case of an erratum the editor has authority to charge the author $60/page if the correction takes up considerable space.

17 CANADIAN PSYCHOLOGIST (1955)

David Gibson, Department of Psychology, The University of Calgary, Calgary, Alberta, T2N 1N4
Publisher & Copyright: Canadian Psychological Association, 1390 Sherbrooke St. W., Montreal 109, Quebec
Subscriptions: $12/yr. (from CPA, Business Office). Quarterly. Ca. 2300. 90 pages/issue.

Special Note: Founded in 1955 as a quarterly and published continuously since. Initiated in 1950 on an irregular basis as a mimeograph. Vol. 1 to IV (part).
Description: "A journal of general psychology including interpretive, theoretical, discipline bridging and mission scholarship, evaluative reviews, comment on psychological affairs and organizational psychology and original research having technological importance."
Intended Audience: Undergraduate, beginning graduate, and advanced graduate students in psychology; academic and community psychologists; teachers; researchers; administrators; practitioners.
Special Features: Theoretical articles; book reviews; edi-

torials; published in English and French; abstract for
each article in both languages; available on microform;
annual index; advertising.

Acceptance/Rejection Criteria: APA style; review panel acceptance; consistent with editorial policy.
Manuscript Disposition: Receipt of MS acknowledged; sent to
two reviewers; returned to author for revision (or rejection); re-circulated to review panel; finally accepted or
rejected; 8 months required for decision; 60% submitted
MSS accepted; 30 MSS published/yr.; 3 issue lag from
acceptance to publication.
Style Requirements: APA Publication Manual; preferred length
10-15 pages, double spaced; 3 copies of MS; abstract required.
Payment: None to or by author for publication.
Reprints: 100 reprints (9-16pp.) approximately $52.00.
Special Note: Editorial policy shifting to bridging, critical
reviews and theory articles.

18   CATALOG OF SELECTED DOCUMENTS IN PSYCHOLOGY
(1971)   Journal Supplement Abstract Service

Executive Editor: Elliot R. Siegel; Journal Supplement Abstract Service, American Psychological Association, 1200
17th Street, N.W., Washington, D.C.   20036
Publisher & Copyright: American Psychological Association
(Journal Supplement Abstract Service).
Subscriptions: $12/yr.   Subscriptions may begin at any time,
but include only that year.   If a subscription is sent in
May, 1974, for example, all 1974 catalogs are sent to
the subscriber.   Quarterly.   Ca. 3000.   At least 40
pages/issue.   Special subscription rate of $5/yr. for
APA members.

Description: "JSAS provides a recognized primary publication channel that bridges the gap between informal communication networks and the journal mode of information
exchange.   JSAS disseminates information on two comple-
mentary levels: descriptive abstracts of materials accepted by the service (which appear in the Catalog) and
separately bound full-text copies of these documents
(which are disseminated by JSAS on a demand basis)."
Article Content: Among the types of documents actively solicited by JSAS are: technical reports; bibliographies;
massive data collections; teaching materials; descriptions

of effective techniques or programs; invited lectures; literature reviews; descriptions of methodological techniques and procedures; discussions of controversial issues; well-designed studies with negative results; major projects in progress.

Typical Disciplines: Psychology and public policy; teaching of psychology; general psychology; methodology and research technology; human experimental psychology; physiological and animal psychology; developmental, social, personality, clinical, educational, personnel & industrial. and engineering psychology.

Special Features: Abstract for each article; contents of volumes available on microform.

Acceptance/Rejection Criteria: Psychology-relevant documents of all types, formats, lengths, and subject matter content are appropriate for JSAS. The only restriction is that the document must not, in its present form, have been formally published elsewhere. Documents accepted by JSAS are of high scientific and technical quality as judged by the JSAS editors and their consulting editors. Standards for acceptance are not measurably different from those used by editors of journals published by the American Psychological Association--except for consideration of the generality of the audience, and for freedom from page limitations and from the traditional requirement for significance of findings.

Manuscript Disposition: Receipt of MS acknowledged; approximately 3 weeks required for decision; rejected MS returned; critique to author; 50-65% submitted MSS accepted, 240 abstracts/yr.; 3 months from acceptance to publication; all documents accepted in time for an issue are published.

Style Requirements: Authors are not limited to using any particular style. They may refer to APA's Publication Manual. No page length requirements. All documents must be submitted directly to JSAS in triplicate and in photo-reproducible or "camera-ready" form. Each document must be accompanied by a 100-300 word descriptive abstract.

Payment: None to or by author.

Reprints: Available at charge.

19   CHANGE (1969) The Magazine of Higher Learning

George W. Bonham, Change Magazine, NBW Tower, New Rochelle, NY   10801

Publisher: George W. Bonham
Subscriptions: $12/yr. Student $8/yr. Issued 10/yr. Ca.
30,000. 64-80 pages/issue.

Description: "Magazine deals almost exclusively with higher
education. It publishes reports on programs, colleges,
conferences and the like as well as more theoretical
analyses of major issues current in the field."
Intended Audience: General public; undergraduate and graduate students in education; teachers; administrators; trustees; researchers; anyone interested in higher education.
Special Features: Research reports; theoretical articles;
columns; book reviews; letters to the editor; editorials;
hortatory or polemical articles; annual index.

Acceptance/Rejection Criteria: MS must deal with some aspect of higher education; major articles, reports and
columns are recognized as three distinctly different types
of work; should be written in a style appropriate to magazine rather than journals; should deal with a fresh subject in a perceptive and imaginative way.
Acceptance/Rejection Procedures: MSS that are inappropriate
are most often returned immediately. Those that seem
to have possibilities are circulated among the editors,
and the author is sent a card saying his MS is being considered.
Manuscript Disposition: 6 weeks required for decision; "blind"
refereeing; 5% submitted articles accepted; 70 MSS pub-
lished/yr.; 3 months from acceptance to publication.
Style Requirements: Reports are approximately 1500-2000
words, major essays are 4000-5000 words; double space;
1 copy of MS; no abstract.
Payment: None by author; authors paid $350 for major ar-
ticles, $150 for reports, $100 for columns.
Reprints: Not available.

20 CHANGING EDUCATION (1966)

David Elsila, American Federation of Teachers, 1012 14th
St. N.W., Washington, D.C. 20005
Publisher: American Federation of Teachers
Subscriptions: $5/yr. Quarterly. Ca. 420,000. 40 pages/
issue.

Description: "A journal aimed at meeting the needs of practicing classroom teachers for information on economic

issues affecting them, on problems of teacher unionism and collective bargaining, on educational trends, and on social issues such as racism in education, academic freedom, and the role of business in education. "

Intended Audience: Classroom teachers.

Special Features: Research reports; theoretical articles; book reviews; letters to the editor; hortatory or polemical articles; literature reviews; available on microform.

Acceptance/Rejection Criteria: Preference given to articles by practicing classroom teachers.

Acceptance/Rejection Procedures: Reading by staff; review by others in field if staff feels this is necessary.

Manuscript Disposition: 6-9 months required for decision; rejected MS returned; 10% submitted MSS accepted; 40 MSS published/yr.; 1 year from acceptance to publication.

Style Requirements: Preferred length 1000 words; maximum 2500 words; 1 copy of MS; no abstract required.

Payment: Authors paid from $25 to $100 for published MSS.

Reprints: Available at cost.

21 COGNITIVE PSYCHOLOGY (1970)

Tom Trabasso, Department of Psychology, Green Hall, Princeton University, Princeton, NJ 08540 [new editor as of Jan. 1, 1975: Earl B. Hunt, Department of Psychology, University of Washington, Seattle, Washington 98105]

Publisher & Copyright: Academic Press, 111 5th Ave., NY 10003

Subscriptions: Indiv. $12/yr. Instit. $36/yr. Bimonthly: 1973 (two vols.). Quarterly: 1974 (one vol.). Ca. 1700. 150 pages/issue.

Description: "Purpose is to publish original empirical, theoretical and tutorial papers, methodological articles and critical reviews dealing with memory, language processing, perception, problem solving and thinking. Emphasis on human information processing. Related areas of linguistics, artificial intelligence and neurophysiology are welcome but must be of direct interest to cognitive psychologists. "

Typical Disciplines: Psychology; linguistics; computer science and artificial intelligence; educational psychology; education.

Intended Audience: Beginning graduate students in psychology; advanced graduate students & specialists; teachers; researchers.

Special Features: Research reports; theoretical articles; literature reviews; abstract for each article; annual index.

Acceptance/Rejection Criteria: Appropriateness of subject; substantial contribution to understanding of mechanisms underlying human information processing; clarity and conciseness of writing; emphasis on seminal and innovative papers of interest primarily to cognitive psychologists.

Acceptance/Rejection Procedures: Main editor decides on appropriateness of content; rejects articles that are obvious candidates for other journals or "second-in-a-series" papers. Editorial board member then becomes "Editor" for paper. He may use outside reviewers. His decision is generally final.

Manuscript Disposition: Receipt of MS acknowledged; two weeks to one month required for rejection decision; two months required on acceptance decision; rejected MS returned; critique to author; 15% submitted MSS accepted; 6-12 months from acceptance to publication; first accepted, first published.

Style Requirements: APA Publication Manual and journal; flexible page length requirements; three copies of MS; page 2 of MS should be abstract of 100-150 words.

Payment: None to author; author charged for major changes on galley proofs.

Reprints: 50 free; additional may be ordered with galley proofs.

22 COLLEGE STUDENT JOURNAL (1966) A Journal Pertaining to College Students
formerly, College Student Survey

Russell N. Cassel, P.O. Box 566, Chula Vista, California 92010

Publisher & Copyright: Project Innovation, 1362 Santa Cruz Court, Chula Vista, CA 92010

Subscriptions: Instit. $10/yr. Indiv. $7.50/yr. Quarterly. Ca. 2000. 100 pages/issue.

Description: "Publishes original papers on theory and research dealing with college student values, attitudes, opinions, and learning, including areas of graduate and professional schools."

Typical Disciplines: Psychology; sociology; education; anthropology.

Intended Audience: Very broad range from general public

through undergraduate and graduate students to teachers, researchers, administrators, and practitioners.

Special Features: Research reports; theoretical articles; book reviews; abstract for each article; annual index; available on microform; Monographs To College Student Journal published from time to time and distributed to subscribers.

Acceptance/Rejection Criteria: MSS judged primarily on basis of originality, freshness, imagination, quality of writing, and timeliness of topic involved.

Manuscript Disposition: Receipt of MS acknowledged; 30 days required for decision; rejected MS returned; 50% submitted MSS accepted; 100 MSS published/yr.; 1 year from acceptance to publication.

Style Requirements: APA Publication Manual, plus guide provided on request; preferred length 1500 to 2500 words; double spacing throughout; 2 copies of MS; abstract required on separate page, should be 100-120 words in length and contain statements of the problem, the method, the results, and conclusions.

Payment: None to author; invited articles, and all articles of 2000 words or less receiving a "Priority" rating by 2 or more members of the editorial board are published without charge; otherwise authors are charged about $5/ typewritten page; authors are also charged for graphs, figures, at minimum rate of about $7, a half page about $10, and a full page about $25.

Reprints: Ordered with galley proofs at nominal charge (i.e., $2/page for 50); authors receive a single complimentary copy of issue containing their article; additional copies of issue available for about $1 each.

23 COLLEGE AND UNIVERSITY (1910) Journal of the American Association of Collegiate Registrars and Admissions Officers

Robert E. Mahn, Office of the Secretary of the University, Ohio University, Athens, Ohio 45701

Publisher & Copyright: American Association of Collegiate Registrars and Admissions Officers

Subscriptions: Included in part of individual and institutional membership. Individual non-member, $8/yr. Quarterly. Ca. 7000. 125 pages/issue with 425 pages/Summer issue, for total of 800 pages.

Description: "Higher Education Journal: Admissions, Regis-
tration, Records, Financial Aids, Institutional Research,
International Educational Relations, Personnel."
Intended Audience: Advanced graduate students and specialists;
researchers; administrators.
Special Features: Research reports; theoretical articles; book
reviews; available on microform; annual and cumulative
index.

Acceptance/Rejection Procedures: Decision of editorial staff.
Manuscript Disposition: Receipt of MS acknowledged; one
month required for decision; rejected MS returned; 10%
submitted MSS accepted; 60 MSS published/yr.; one quar-
ter from acceptance to publication; first accepted, first
published.
Style Requirements: No exact format specified--see journal;
preferred length 10 pages, double spaced; no minimum,
maximum length 20 pages; 1 copy of MS; abstract not
required.
Payment: None to or by authors.
Reprints: Available; charge determined by printer.

24 COLORADO JOURNAL OF EDUCATIONAL RESEARCH
(1962)
formerly, Journal of Research Services

D. W. Chaloupka, Bureau of Research, 529 McKee, Univer-
sity of Northern Colorado, Greeley, CO 80631
Publisher & Copyright: Same as above.
Subscriptions: Institit. $6/yr. Indiv. $1.50/yr. Quarterly.
Ca. 2500. 56 pages/issue.

Description: "Publishes educational research conducted in
Colorado and selected papers from the University of
Northern Colorado."
Intended Audience: Teachers; researchers; administrators;
students.
Special Features: Research reports; special theme for some
issues.

Acceptance/Rejection Criteria: Research must originate in
Colorado.
Acceptance/Rejection Procedures: No formal procedures; re-
view by editor.
Manuscript Disposition: Receipt of MS acknowledged; one
month required for decision; research reports only; 20 MSS

published/yr.; 3 months from acceptance to publication.
Style Requirements: Write editor for guidelines; no stated
page length; 2 copies of MS; abstract not required.
Payment: None to or by author.
Reprints: Available at charge.

25 COMMUNICATION RESEARCH (1974) An International
Quarterly

F. Gerald Kline, Department of Journalism, Room 2040J,
L. S. & A. Bldg., University of Michigan, Ann Arbor,
MI 48104
Publisher & Copyright: Sage Publications, Inc., 275 So.
Beverly Drive, Beverly Hills, CA 90212
Subscriptions: Instit. $18/yr. Indiv. $12/yr. Student $9/
yr. Quarterly. 128 pages/issue.

Description: "Will be concerned with the study of communication processes at all levels. Within this field's rapidly
expanding boundaries, the journal will focus on explication
and testing of models that explain the processes and outcomes of communication. "
Typical Disciplines: Journal has a wide scope, including such
fields as psychology, journalism, political science, economics, sociology, marketing and speech communication.
A major goal is the unification of common communication
interests across these and other fields.
Intended Audience: Beginning graduate students in psychology;
advanced graduate students & specialists; teachers; researchers; administrators; practitioners.
Special Features: Research reports; theoretical articles;
book reviews; letters to the editor; annual index; advertising.

Acceptance/Rejection Criteria: MSS submitted should provide
theoretical contributions derived from supporting data that
meet specific standards. If these requirements are met,
the editors will accept articles using whatever theoretical
or methodological approaches are appropriate to the author's purposes. Emphasis will be placed on quality, not
on orthodoxy.
Acceptance/Rejection Procedures: MSS will be subjected to
a rigorous system of refereeing in an attempt to meet
the highest standards of scientific endeavor in comparable
fields. In addition, contributors will be actively sought
from varying perspectives on communication, whether they

stem from disciplinary, philosophical, or geographical diversity.

Manuscript Disposition: Receipt of MS acknowledged; "blind" refereeing; rejected MS returned; critique to author.

Style Requirements: Available from editor or publisher, also see journal; preferred length 15-25 pages, double spaced; 3 copies of MS; abstract required.

Payment: None to or by author.

Reprints: 24 free; charge for additional copies depends on article length.

26 COMPACT (1966)

Robert L. Jacobson, Managing Editor, Education Commission of the States, 300 Lincoln Tower, 1860 Lincoln St., Denver, CO 80203

Publisher & Copyright: Education Commission of the States.

Subscriptions: $6/yr. Bimonthly. 15,000. 32-48 pages/issue.

Description: A magazine covering state-related activities in education.

Article Content: All levels and aspects of education, with special attention to state legislation and administration.

Intended Audience: State officials and legislators; educators; researchers; administrators; practitioners.

Special Features: Book reviews; letters to the editor; annual index.

Acceptance/Rejection Criteria: Informative and highly readable reports of state-related education activities.

Manuscript Disposition: Queries welcome; no unsolicited manuscripts.

Style Requirements: Wire service style manual; typical length of featured articles--800 to 1500 words.

Payment: Varies.

Reprints: Rates available on request.

27 CONDITIONAL REFLEX (1966) A Pavlovian Journal of Research & Therapy
[New title, 1974: THE PAVLOVIAN JOURNAL OF BIOLOGICAL SCIENCE]

W. Horsley Gantt, Pavlovian Research Laboratory, VA Hospital, Perry Point, MD 21902

Publisher & Copyright: J. B. Lippincott Co.
Organizational Affiliation: Pavlovian Society
Subscriptions: Indiv. $20/yr. Quarterly. 65 pages/issue.

Description: "An international journal for dissemination of
knowledge in the fields of research in normal and abnormal, human and animal behavior."
Article Content: Original articles pertaining to the experimental analysis of human and animal behavior. Also
theoretical and review papers based on observational data.
Intended Audience: Students in psychology and education;
teachers; researchers; practitioners; those in psychophysi-
ology.
Special Features: Research reports; theoretical articles;
book reviews; editorials; apparatus section for short communication describing devices and procedures related to
the Pavlovian research technique; abstracts of papers at
annual Pavlovian Society meetings; publication of special
symposia held at annual Pavlovian Society meetings; publication of Pavlovian Society Award papers; abstract for
each article; annual index.

Acceptance/Rejection Criteria: Length of article; value of
research results; literary presentation.
Acceptance/Rejection Procedures: Articles are sent to editors (more than one) for review; editorial comments
(sans name of editor) are sent to the author; MSS are
either rejected or accepted on the basis of editorial review; on occasion several opinions are obtained when
there appears to be controversy.
Manuscript Disposition: Receipt of MS acknowledged; rejected
MS returned; critique to author; 70% submitted MSS accepted; 30 MSS published/yr.; 3-6 months from acceptance
to publication.
Style Requirements: Consult journal; preferred length 15
pages, double spaced, 1 1/2 inch margin on all sides;
3 copies of MS; abstract of not more than 250 words.
Payment: None to or by authors for publication.
Reprints: Ordered at charge from publisher.

28 CONTEMPORARY EDUCATION (1929)
formerly, Teachers College Journal

M. Dale Baughman, School of Education, 118 N. Sixth St.,
Indiana State University, Terre Haute, IN 47809
Publisher & Copyright: School of Education, Indiana State
University.

Subscriptions: $7/yr. Quarterly (beginning 1973-74; previously 6 times/yr.). Ca. 3600. 68 pages/issue.

Description: "Purpose is to publish discussions of contemporary problems in education. "
Article Content: Contemporary problems in education; special education; reading; curriculum; accountability; student teaching; administration and supervision.
Intended Audience: Readers include professors, students, inservice professionals, administrators and non-educators.
Special Features: Research reports; book reviews; editorials; special theme for some issues; annual index; available on microfilm.

Acceptance/Rejection Criteria: Timely topic; relevant to scope of journal; MSS for theme issues solicited by guest editor, generally.
Acceptance/Rejection Procedures: MSS sent to editorial associates for evaluation; returned to editorial office where decision made to accept or reject.
Manuscript Disposition: Receipt of MS acknowledged; 2 months required for decision; rejected MS returned (stamped, self-addressed envelope should accompany MSS); critique to author; 20% submitted MSS accepted; 40 to 50 MSS published/yr.; 6-12 months from acceptance to publication; policy usually first accepted, first published.
Style Requirements: Available from editor; preferred length 10-12 pages, double spaced; minimum 2, maximum 15 pages; 1 copy of MS; abstract not required.
Payment: None by author; author gets royalty fee of $12.50 for an article that a commercial publication wishes to use.
Reprints: May be obtained by writing Dr. Baughman.

29 CONTEMPORARY PSYCHOLOGY (1956) A Journal of Reviews

Janet T. Spence, Department of Psychology, The University of Texas at Austin, Austin, TX 78712
Publisher & Copyright: American Psychological Association, 1200 17th St., N.W., Washington, D.C. 20036
Subscriptions: $15/yr. Available on calendar-year (Jan.-Dec.) basis. Monthly. Ca. 8700. 64 pages/issue.

Description: "A journal of reviews--critical reviews--of books, films and other material in the field of psychology

and related behavioral sciences. Material represents
world-wide cross-section. "

Intended Audience: Psychologists; psychiatrists; anthropolo-
gists; sociologists; philosophers; persons working in government, industry, and business, and the people who like
to know what is going on in new thinking in psychology.

Special Features: Book reviews; letters to the editor (when
a reader or author feels that a particular review is un-
satisfactory, he may submit a letter presenting the evidence for this conclusion to be published in On the Other
Hand); annual index.

Acceptance/Rejection Procedures: Almost all books to be
reviewed are supplied by publishers; books sent to various advisory editors with request that consultant decide
whether the book should be reviewed, briefly noted, or
not reviewed; if to be reviewed, consultant indicates a
recommended length, beginning with 500 words and rang-
ing upward in units of 500 words (1000 words is average);
advisory editor is also asked to list, in order of preference, recommended reviewers; editor reviews these
recommendations, and, once approved, potential reviewers are invited to prepare the review until there is an
acceptance; two reviewers may be assigned for volumes
of unusual significance; volunteer reviews or volunteer
reviewers for a particular book are not accepted.

30 THE COUNSELING PSYCHOLOGIST (1969)

Dr. John M. Whiteley, Dean of Students, University of California, Irvine, CA 92664

Publisher & Copyright: Division of Counseling Psychology of
the American Psychological Association.

Subscriptions: Instit. $12/yr. Indiv. $10/yr. Student $8/
yr. Order from: Box 1180, Washington University, St.
Louis, MO 63130. Quarterly. Ca. 4000. 100 pages/
issue.

Description: "To provide in-depth, intensive study of particular topics in the counseling psychology field, as presented
by authorities on the topic. A publication of critical review and evaluation of important professional issues. "

Article Content: Client-centered therapy; integrity groups;
counseling women; new directions in training; behavioral,
vocational, existential, and family counseling.

Intended Audience: Psychologists and counselors in schools,

colleges, and universities, public and private agencies, business and industry.

Special Features: The format consists of a lead article written by a distinguished contributor, followed by a series of reviews and critiques. The author of the lead article then has an opportunity for a rejoinder. Also a forum for discussion of these topics, reviews of the literature on topics of importance, and brief reports of innovative professional practices in counseling psychology.

Acceptance/Rejection Criteria: Majority of articles are solicited, to give balance and coverage on the specific topic for that issue.

Acceptance/Rejection Procedures: Read by Editor, Managing Editor and/or Asst. Man. Editor, and by members of Editorial Board if appropriate.

Manuscript Disposition: MSS submitted to The Counseling Psychologist, Box 1180, Washington University, St. Louis, MO 63130; receipt of MS acknowledged; 50 MSS published/ yr.; 4-6 months from acceptance to publication.

Style Requirements: APA Publication Manual; preferred length 10 pages, double spaced; emphasis on topic, not length; 3 copies of MS required; no abstract.

Payment: None to or by author for publication.

Reprints: Author receives some complimentary copies of whole journal.

31 COUNSELING AND VALUES (1956)
    formerly, National Catholic Guidance Conference Journal

Donald A. Biggs, 332 Walter Library, University of Minnesota, Minneapolis, MN 55455

Publisher & Copyright: National Catholic Guidance Conference (A Division of the American Personnel and Guidance Association).

Subscriptions: $8/yr. Order from Executive Director, Willis E. Bartlett, Department of Graduate Studies in Education, University of Notre Dame, Notre Dame, IN 46556. Quarterly. Ca. 1500. 70 pages/issue.

Description: "A professional journal of theory, research, and informed opinion about problems and issues in guidance, counseling, student personnel administration, and supporting psychological services in educational institutions and school-related agencies."

Intended Audience: Counselors; teachers; researchers;

administrators; practitioners.

Special Features: Special theme for each issue; articles inclined theoretically, philosophically, empirically, or methodologically; annual index; advertising.

Acceptance/Rejection Criteria: MSS evaluated on both content and style; primarily interested in articles which are concerned with the interphase between values and counseling programs; accepts articles of a practical nature.

Acceptance/Rejection Procedures: All MSS anonymously reviewed by two consultants.

Manuscript Disposition: Receipt of MS acknowledged; three weeks required for decision; "blind" refereeing; rejected MS returned; critique to author; 40% submitted MSS accepted; 40 MSS published/yr.; about 18 months from acceptance to publication; first accepted, first published.

Style Requirements: APA Publication Manual; preferred length ten pages, double spaced; minimum 2 pages, maximum length 15 pages; 2 copies of MS; no abstract.

Payment: None to or by author for publication.

Reprints: Available at charge.

32 DAEDALUS (1958)

Stephen R. Graubard, 7 Linden Street, Harvard University, Cambridge, MA 02138

Publisher & Copyright: American Academy of Arts and Sciences.

Subscriptions: $10/yr. Quarterly. Ca. 65,000. 250 pages/issue.

Description: "Each issue of Daedalus is devoted to a specific topic. Its primary purpose is to apply interdisciplinary thought to major problems and intellectual concerns of the day."

Intended Audience: Very broad range from general public through advanced graduate students to faculty, researchers, administrators.

Special Features: Special theme each issue; annual index; available on microform.

Acceptance/Rejection Criteria: Only articles commissioned by the editors printed. Authors paid $500 to $1000 per article. 55 MSS published/yr.

33 DEVELOPMENTAL PSYCHOLOGY (1969)

Richard D. Odom, Psychology Dept., Vanderbilt Univ., Nashville, TN 37203
Publisher & Copyright: American Psychological Association,
1200 17th Street, N.W., Washington, D.C. 20036
Subscriptions: Instit. & Indiv. $30/yr. Available on a Jan.-
Dec. basis only. Bimonthly. Ca. 4000. 160 pages/
issue.

Description: "Devoted mostly to research articles pertaining
to all segments of the life span for human beings and
animals, although most articles are concerned with human beings."
Article Content: Contains articles which represent the broad
range of growth and development and their major asso-
ciated variables; chronological age as well as sex, socio-
economic status and effects of physical growth are all
relevant variables; cross-species articles and articles
concerning developmental research with retardates also
included.
Intended Audience: Undergraduate, beginning and advanced
graduate students in psychology; teachers; researchers;
practitioners.
Special Features: Research reports; theoretical articles;
occasional editorials; brief reports and notes (which are
given early publication); volume index, semi-annual; advertising.

Acceptance/Rejection Criteria: Excellence of article; developmental relevance; importance of topic.
Acceptance/Rejection Procedures: Some MSS sent to Associate Editor, who is autonomous, others stay with Editor;
MSS read, edited, and in most cases sent to a Consulting Editor; if there is agreement, MS is accepted; if
not, MS is sent to another Consulting Editor and majority
opinion decides.
Manuscript Disposition: Receipt of MS acknowledged; one
month from receipt to decision; "blind" refereeing; rejected MS returned; critique to author; 22% submitted
MSS accepted; 117 MSS published/yr.; 6-8 months from
acceptance to publication; first received, first published.
Style Requirements: APA Publication Manual, journal; no
maximum, but preferred length 10-20 pages, double
spaced; 2 copies of MS; abstract required.
Payment: None to or by author for publication.
Reprints: Available at charge.

34 EDUCATION (1880)

Russell N. Cassel, Box 566, Chula Vista, California 92010
Publisher & Copyright: Project Innovation, 1362 Santa Cruz
  Court, Chula Vista, CA 92010
Subscriptions: Instit. $10/yr. Indiv. $7.50/yr. Quarterly.
  Ca. 4000. 100 pages/issue.

Description: "Publishes original investigations and theoretical
  papers dealing with worthwhile innovations in learning,
  teaching, and education. Journal's primary concern is
  with teacher education in all its many aspects. Preference also given to innovations in schools."
Article Content: Papers concern all levels and every area of
  education and learning.
Intended Audience: Educators; teachers; students; researchers;
  practitioners.
Special Features: Research reports; theoretical articles;
  book reviews; abstract for each article; issue devoted to
  Margaret Mead, April, 1974; annual index; available on
  microform.

Acceptance/Rejection Criteria: Originality and freshness;
  timeliness of topic; papers both proposed or actual and
  theoretical or evaluative accepted.
Acceptance/Rejection Procedures: Editorial Board members
  consulted for questionable MSS.
Manuscript Disposition: Receipt of MS acknowledged; 30 days
  required for decision; rejected MS returned; 50% submitted MSS accepted; 100 MSS published/yr.; 1 year
  from acceptance to publication.
Style Requirements: Guide furnished on request, see also
  APA Manual; preferred length 4-5 pages, double spaced
  or 2000 words; 2 copies of MS; abstract required on
  separate page, should be 100-120 words in length and
  contain statements of the problem, the method, the results, and conclusions.
Payment: None to author; invited articles, and all articles
  of 2000 words or less receiving a "Priority" rating by
  2 or more members of the Editorial Board are published
  without charge; otherwise authors are charged about $12/
  typewritten page; authors also charged for graphs and
  figures at a minimum rate of $7, half page about $12,
  and full page about $25.
Reprints: Ordered with galley proofs at nominal charge (i.e.,
  $2/page for 50); authors receive a single complimentary
  copy of issue containing their article, additional copies of
  issue available for about $1 each.

35 EDUCATION CANADA (1945)
    formerly Canadian Education & Research Digest

Harriett Goldsborough, Canadian Education Association, 252
    Bloor St. West, Toronto, Ontario, Canada M5S 1V5
Publisher & Copyright: Canadian Education Association.
Subscriptions: Instit. $5/yr. Indiv. member $10/yr. (in-
    cludes monthly newsletter and annual publication of CEA
    convention proceedings). Available on calendar year
    basis only. Quarterly. Ca. 4500. 48 pages/issue.

Description: "Editorial objective is to serve as a forum for
    thoughtful expression of views on issues and problems
    of practical concern to readers. Publication fills an im-
    portant role between scholarly research journals and the
    various commercial magazines--less formal than the
    former, more formal than the latter."
Article Content: Elementary and secondary school practices,
    trends, programs and philosophies of interest to Cana-
    dian senior administrative school officials and department
    of education officials.
Intended Audience: Senior persons responsible for policy and
    administration in urban school systems, provincial De-
    partments of Education, and teacher training institutions
    in Canada.
Special Features: Research reports (a few); book reviews;
    hortatory or polemical articles; annual index; available
    on microform.

Acceptance/Rejection Criteria: Over half of the MSS are re-
    quested from particular Canadian educators writing on a
    requested topic; writing should be contemporary and inter-
    esting; remember that the publication's readers are con-
    fronted with quite practical problems; present relevant
    material in a clear, concise and easy-to-read style; ar-
    ticle may be based on a specific program or project, and
    related closely to it, but approach should be analytical--
    commenting and giving opinions about implications and out-
    comes, rather than enumerating activities only; article
    may be based on research findings, but emphasis should
    be on the practical implications of the conclusions or find-
    ings.
Manuscript Disposition: Receipt of MS acknowledged; 3 months
    required for decision on unsolicited MSS; rejected MS re-
    turned; 20% submitted MSS accepted; 32 MSS published/
    yr.; 4 weeks to 3 months from acceptance to publication.
Style Requirements: Guidelines available from editor; generally

shortest articles about 1500 words; preferred length 3000 words; maximum length 4000 words; 2 copies of MS; no abstract; photos welcome.

Payment: None to or by authors.
Reprints: Not available.

36 EDUCATION AND URBAN SOCIETY (1968)

Jay D. Scribner (UCLA)
Editorial Address: Managing Editor, Education and Urban Society, Sage Publications, 275 South Beverly Drive, Beverly Hills, CA 90212
Publisher & Copyright: Sage Publications
Subscriptions: Instit. $18/yr. Indiv. $10/yr. Student $9/yr. Quarterly. 128 pages/issue.

Description: "During recent years an increasing number of social scientists have been conducting research on education as a social institution. Research studies have not been limited to the working of the institution however, but have begun to explore educational institutions and processes as agents of social change. Much of this work, of course, centers on the problems and needs resulting from the national concern with improving the urban environment, but also involves the role of education in a society which is urban. This journal exists to foster such research and to provide a multidisciplinary forum for communication."

Article Content: Measurement of effects of teacher training; segregation; organizational change; citizens' attitudes.

Typical Disciplines: Education and psychology; administrators involved in public policy decision making.

Intended Audience: Broad range from general public through undergraduate and graduate students to researchers and administrators.

Special Features: Research reports; theoretical articles; book reviews; review essays; literature reviews; annual index; advertising.

Acceptance/Rejection Procedures: Each appropriate MS sent to 2 members of the editorial advisory board; judgments pooled by the editor; editor makes the final decision.

Manuscript Disposition: Receipt of MS acknowledged; 6-8 weeks required for decision; "blind" refereeing; rejected MS returned; 30-40% submitted MSS accepted; 30-40 MSS published/yr.; 6-9 months from acceptance to publication;

first accepted, first published.

Style Requirements: Available upon request from editor or publisher. Preferred length 25-30 pages, double spaced; 3 copies of MS; no abstract.

Payment: None to or by author.

Reprints: 24 without charge; additional charge depends on article length.

37 EDUCATIONAL ADMINISTRATION QUARTERLY (1966)

Fred D. Carver, 314 Education Building, University of Illinois, Urbana, IL 61801

Publisher & Copyright: University Council for Educational Administration, 29 West Woodruff Ave., Columbus, OH 43210

Subscriptions: Indiv. $7.50/yr. or $18/3 yrs. Full-time graduate students $4/yr. Issued 3/yr. Ca. 1900. 100 pages/issue.

Description: "Purpose to provide for discourse and dialogue among students of educational administration. There is a major focus on theoretical considerations in the selection of content. Empirical studies are acceptable providing their presentation includes significant conceptual frameworks. Also acceptable are pieces on important value and policy questions. All levels of the educational enterprise are encompassed and no restrictions are placed on the type of administrative organization that may be represented."

Article Content: Theoretical, empirical, analytical, synthesis and policy pieces related to organizational arrangements, administrator behavior, organizational or management climate, change, legal aspects, finance, systems analysis, motivation, communication, decision making, and collective bargaining.

Typical Disciplines: Educ. Admin. & Supervision; Teacher Educ.; Special Ed. Admin.; El. & Sec. Ed.; Ed. Psych.; Ed. Policy Studies; Higher Ed.; Social Psych.; History and Phil. of Ed.; Pol. Sci.; Sociology.

Intended Audience: Practicing administrators interested in scholarly development of the field; professors and graduate students in educational administration; other social scientists.

Special Features: Research reports; theoretical articles; book reviews; editorials; hortatory or polemical articles; abstract for each article; annual index; available on microform; one invited MS included/issue.

Acceptance/Rejection Criteria: Significance and timeliness of content; quality of research (if research article); quality of writing; contribution to knowledge in educational administration or to practice specifically.

Acceptance/Rejection Procedure: Two copies sent, without author identification, for referee reaction on the part of at least two members of the editorial board or other specialists in the area of concern. On the basis of these reports and the judgment of the editorial staff, MSS are considered to be either acceptable for publication, worthy of revision, or rejected as unsuitable for a variety of reasons. If accepted as suitable for publication they are placed in competition with other accepted articles in the making up of a specific issue.

Manuscript Disposition: Receipt of MS acknowledged; 6 weeks required for decision; "blind" refereeing; rejected MS returned (one copy only); critique to author; 10% submitted MSS accepted; 15-16 MSS published/yr.; 4 months from acceptance to publication.

Style Requirements: Consult journal; preferred length 15-20 pages, double spaced; 3 copies of MS; cover page should give title, authors and positions, and a 50-word lead-in to the article; title of article repeated at beginning of text on next page, but there should be no further identification of authors; footnotes at end of MS, follow Turabian's A Manual for Writers.

Payment: None to or by author for publication.

Reprints: 25 free; about $25 for 1st 25, $4.25 for each additional 25.

38 EDUCATIONAL HORIZONS (1921)
formerly, Pi Lambda Theta Journal

Mrs. Miriam M. Bryan, Educational Testing Service, Suite 100, 17 Executive Drive, N.W., Atlanta, Georgia 30329

Publisher & Copyright: Pi Lambda Theta, 200 E. 8th St., Bloomington, Indiana 47401

Subscriptions: Instit. & Indiv. $5/yr. Included in members' dues. Quarterly. Ca. 16,000. 50 pages/issue.

Description: "Purpose is to foster creativity and academic excellence; support, extend, and interpret the function of education in a democracy; stimulate research; aid evaluation and improvement of the profession of teaching; contribute to the solution of educational, social, and cultural problems of national and international concern; and

promote professional fellowship and cooperation. "
Article Content: Any current topic in any aspect of education.
Intended Audience: Teachers; administrators; practitioners;
   students in education.
Special Features: Research reports; theoretical articles;
   special theme for each issue; will be available on microform.

Acceptance/Rejection Criteria: Report should not be highly
   statistical in nature.
Acceptance/Rejection Procedures: MS is submitted to the
   editor; if there is a guest editor for the issue, the MS
   is also sent to the guest editor.
Manuscript Disposition: Receipt of MS acknowledged; 6 months
   required for decision (due to single theme per issue); rejected MS returned, if requested; 30 MSS published/yr.;
   6 months from acceptance to publication (each issue is
   centered around a theme so a MS may be held until such
   time as related theme is used).
Style Requirements: Consult journal; preferred length less
   than 1500 words; one copy of MS; abstract not required.
Payment: None to or by author.
Reprints: Charge based upon cost of reprinting.

39 EDUCATIONAL LEADERSHIP (1943)

Robert R. Leeper, Association for Supervision & Curriculum
   Development, 1701 K Street, N.W., Suite 1100, Washington, D.C. 20006
Publisher & Copyright: Association for Supervision & Curriculum Development
Subscriptions: $8/yr. Issued 8/yr. in October-May. Ca.
   18,000. 100 pages/issue.

Description: "The contents of this journal are directed to all
   persons interested in improving instruction. It provides
   an open forum for the free expression of competent opinion. "
Article Content: Articles in each issue are usually organized
   around a theme based upon the expressed interests and
   concerns of the ASCD membership. Upcoming themes
   are published in advance in a call for MSS.
Intended Audience: Supervisors; curriculum specialists; teachers; principals; education teachers and students; school
   superintendents; directors of instruction; consultants.
Special Features: Research reports; theoretical articles; book

reviews; letters to the editor; editorials; special theme
each issue; news notes; annual index; advertising.

Manuscript Disposition: 2 weeks required for decision; rejected MS returned.
Style Requirements: Preferred length 5 pages double spaced
or 1400 words; maximum length 6 pages or 1500 words;
1 or 2 copies of MS; no abstract.
Payment: None to or by authors.
Reprints: Information provided to authors.

40 EDUCATIONAL PERSPECTIVES (1961)

Dr. Alex L. Pickens, University of Hawaii, College of Edu-
cation, Wist Annex 2, 223-D, 1776 University Avenue,
Honolulu, HI 96822
Publisher & Copyright: University of Hawaii
Subscriptions: Instit. & Indiv. $2/yr. Quarterly. Ca. 1000.
32 pages/issue.

Description: "Professional education journal. Each issue
deals with specific issue/curriculum area in education.
Both local and national contributors."
Article Content: Teaching of language; special education;
counseling & guidance; health, science, art education.
Intended Audience: Curriculum specialists; classroom teachers; higher education professionals; administrators; students; general and college-educated public.
Special Features: Special theme each issue; cumulative index;
only education journal in Pacific area.

Acceptance/Rejection Criteria: Any topical MS is acceptable
for consideration. Most issues of journal center around
a single theme. Excellent articles, however, are used
as often as possible even though they deviate from theme.
Reworked speeches are acceptable, but reprints from
other publications not acceptable.
Manuscript Disposition: Receipt of MS acknowledged; 3 weeks
required for decision; "blind" refereeing; rejected MS returned; critique to author; 15% submitted MSS accepted;
28-30 MSS published/yr.; 6-9 months from acceptance
to publication.
Style Requirements: See journal; preferred length 2500 to
3000 words; MS pages double spaced; abstract not required; subheads are desirable; MSS should be documented,
footnoted, and bibliographies included where needed; suit-

able visual material--photographs are desirable; a brief
biographical sketch of each author is needed; a photo-
graph of each author (to accompany biographical data) is
optional.

Payment: None to or by author.

Reprints: 3 copies of the issue in which his article appears
are sent to the author; reprints may be ordered from
printer.

41 EDUCATIONAL AND PSYCHOLOGICAL MEASUREMENT

Dr. W. Scott Gehman, Box 6907, College Station, Durham,
North Carolina 27708

Copyright: Frederic Kuder

Subscriptions: $16/yr. Quarterly. 230 pages/issue.

Description: "Devoted to the development and application of
measures of individual differences."

Article Content: Discussions of problems in the field of
measurement of individual differences; reports of research on development and use of tests and measurement
in education, industry, and government; descriptions of
testing programs being used for various purposes; mis-
cellaneous notes pertinent to measurement field such as
suggestions of new types of items or improved methods
of treating test data.

Special Features: Computer programs; book reviews.

Style Requirements: APA Publication Manual; 2 copies of
MS; abstract not required; tables and footnotes on separate pages; journal titles are not abbreviated.

Payment: None to authors; authors' charges approximately
$30/page of running text and $40/page of tables, figures,
formulas.

Reprints: Authors granted permission to have reprints made
of own articles for own use at own expense.

42 EDUCATIONAL RECORD (1920)
formerly, The Educational Record

Clifford B. Fair, Educational Record, American Council on
Education, One Dupont Circle, Washington, D.C. 20036

Publisher & Copyright: American Council on Education

Subscriptions: $10/yr. Quarterly. Ca. 10,000. 80-90
pages/issue.

Description: "Concerned with the broad range of issues affecting contemporary higher education, this journal provides a platform for the presentation of ideas and information of importance to colleges and universities in
the United States."
Article Content: Governance; organization; discrimination;
curriculum; planning; federal and state relations.
Intended Audience: Teachers; researchers; administrators.
Special Features: Research reports; theoretical articles;
book reviews; editorials; hortatory or polemical articles;
cumulative index.

Acceptance/Rejection Criteria: Interest and significance in
higher education; quality of writing; timeliness.
Acceptance/Rejection Procedures: The editor makes the decision for acceptance or rejection based upon the judgment
of two or three readers, usually members of the Council's Executive Staff.
Manuscript Disposition: Receipt of MS acknowledged; 3 months
required for decision; "blind" refereeing; rejected MS returned; 15% submitted MSS accepted; 50 MSS published/
yr.; 3 months from acceptance to publication.
Style Requirements: Guide available on request; preferred
length 12-18 pages, double spaced; no minimum; maximum length 20 pages; one copy of MS; no abstract.
Payments: None to or by author for publication.
Reprints: 100 free; additional available for charge.

43 EDUCATIONAL RESEARCH (1958)

Editors, Educational Research, NFER, The Mere, Upton
Park, Slough, Bucks, England
Publisher & Copyright: National Foundation for Educational
Research in England and Wales
Subscriptions: Address APA Publications, Inc., 150 Fifth
Avenue, New York, NY 10011. Issued 3 times/yr.
Ca. 4000. 80 pages/issue.

Description: "A review for teachers and all concerned with
education. Original research investigations, evaluative
reviews of recent research in particular areas of education, or discussion articles on research topics accepted."
Intended Audience: Educationists in general; teachers; researchers; administrators; students.
Special Features: Research reports; theoretical articles;
book reviews; literature reviews; abstract for each article;

occasional letters to the editor and editorials; cumulative
index (once in 3 years); advertising.

Acceptance/Rejection Criteria: Originality of research, validity, significance; coherence and completeness; relevance
to educationists in general, and ordinary intelligent teachers; application of findings (what can reader do with results?); co-ordination, interpretation, criticism of relevant research in area; avoidance of technical jargon; suitability of style for intended audience.
Acceptance/Rejection Procedures: MSS read by members of
the parent organization (NFER); editor makes final decision.
Manuscript Disposition: Receipt of MS acknowledged; 6 months
required for decision; rejected MS returned; critique to
author where possible; 1 in 3 MSS accepted; 40 MSS pub-
lished/yr.; 6 months from acceptance to publication; generally first accepted, first published.
Style Requirements: Request guidelines from editor and consult journal; preferred length 10 pages double spaced or
3000 words; 2 copies of MS; should have very brief in-
troductory summary; references in the text should be in
the form of the author's surname and the year of publication only, in brackets, inserted at the appropriate place;
alphabetical bibliography with full details, at the end of
MS; define key terminology.
Payment: None to or by author.
Reprints: 25 free; additional available at charge.

44   EDUCATIONAL RESEARCHER (1972)

Richard Schutz, (SWRL Educational Research and Development),
4665 Lampson Ave., Los Alamitos, CA 90720
Publisher & Copyright: American Educational Research Asso-
ciation, 1126 16th St., N.W., Washington, D.C. 20036
Subscriptions: $10/yr. Free with AERA membership.
Monthly. Ca. 11,000. 32 pages/issue.

Description: "Provides a forum for educational research and
development. In addition to staff-written material, publishes the following types of articles: (1) Articles. Analyses or syntheses of scholarly inquiry written in a narrative style. (2) Essay-Reviews of publications dealing with
the significance of the work to the field of educational research. (3) Brief notes or commentary on issues, events,
or developments in educational research. (4) Letters on

matters of both general and specialized interest to educational researchers. "

Typical Disciplines: Academic social sciences.

Intended Audience: Very broad range from general public, undergraduate and graduate students to teachers, researchers, administrators and practitioners.

Special Features: Theoretical articles; book reviews; letters to the editor; editorials; AERA annual reports and news; professional activities section; employment advertising; available on microform.

Acceptance/Rejection Criteria: Articles should emphasize interpretations and implications for research and development in education. Essay-reviews must not be limited to commentary on the contents, structure, thesis or validity of the work. MSS should be carefully organized in a logical sequence. Write in narrative style and reasonably nontechnical language, avoiding excessive jargon. When possible, write in the active voice, using the first person. MSS should not be under consideration by another publisher.

Acceptance/Rejection Procedures: Authors should include with MS suggestions of two to four appropriate referees who are not affiliated with the author's institution; MSS are reviewed by one or more referees in speciality appropriate to the subject.

Manuscript Disposition: Receipt of MS acknowledged; author nominates referees; 3 weeks required for decision; rejected MS returned; critique to author; 75 MSS published/ yr.; 2 months from acceptance to publication; first accepted, first published.

Style Requirements: Follow recognized general style manual, such as The University of Chicago Press Manual of Style; also see Jan. 1972 issue of journal, and request "Instructions to Contributors"; articles range from 2000 to 5000 words; letters from 200 to 300; double space; 3 copies of MS; no abstract; send letter of transmission with MS and include a brief statement of the subject and scope of the article and suggestions for referees.

Payment: None to or by author for publication.

45 EDUCATIONAL RESOURCES & TECHNIQUES

Ralph Holloway, Eastfield College, 3737 Motley Dr., Mesquite, TX 75149

Publisher & Copyright: Texas Association for Educational Technology

Subscriptions: Institutional (Associate Membership) $7/yr.
Individual member (active) $12/yr. Service Member
$20/yr. Subscriptions available on calendar-year basis
only. Back issues will be sent if one joins before Aug.
1. Membership runs from November 1 to November 1.
Quarterly. Ca. 1000. 36 pages/issue.

Description: "Primary purpose is to keep members abreast
of educational technology as it applies to their own interest. Designed for educators."
Typical Disciplines: Librarians; Media Specialists; Instructional Developers; Educational Technologists.
Intended Audience: Undergraduate and graduate students in
education; teachers; researchers; administrators; practitioners.
Special Features: Editorials; special theme each issue; annual and cumulative index; available on microform; advertising.

Acceptance/Rejection Criteria: MSS are accepted or rejected
on the basis of their content and how it relates to the interest of journal's audience.
Acceptance/Rejection Procedures: MSS are sent to editor or
editorial board. All final decisions are the editor's.
Manuscript Disposition: Receipt of MS acknowledged; 2 weeks
required for decision; rejected MS returned; 95% submitted MSS accepted; 20 MSS published/yr.; 3 months
from acceptance to publication.
Style Requirements: Statement available from editor; preferred length 3500 words; no minimum, maximum length;
1 copy of MS; no abstract.
Payment: None to or by author.
Reprints: 2 copies of journal provided free; $2.50 per addi-
tional copy of journal.

46 EDUCATIONAL TECHNOLOGY

Lawrence Lipsitz, 140 Sylvan Ave., Englewood Cliffs, New
Jersey 07632
Publisher & Copyright: Educational Technology Publications,
Inc., 140 Sylvan Ave., Englewood Cliffs, NJ 07632
Subscriptions: $21/yr. Monthly. 65 pages/issue.

Description: "The magazine for managers of change in education. Covers educational technology in two broad cate-
gories--technology-as-machines and technology-as-applied
science."

Special Features: Book reviews; special theme for some issues; news notes; advertising; available on microform.

Acceptance/Rejection Criteria: Subscribers invited to submit articles, letters, reviews, and reports. Enclose stamped return evelope with all MSS.

47 ENVIRONMENT AND BEHAVIOR (1969) An Interdisciplinary journal

Gary H. Winkel, Environmental Psychology Program, City University of New York, 33 W. 42nd St., New York, NY 10036
Publisher & Copyright: Sage Publications, Inc., 275 So. Beverly Drive, Beverly Hills, CA 90212
Subscriptions: Instit. $20/yr. Indiv. $12/yr. Student $9/yr. Quarterly. 128 pages/issue.

Description: "This journal was brought into being to report rigorous experimental and theoretical work focusing on the influence of the physical environment on human behavior at the individual, group, and institutional levels."
Article Content: Theoretical work on human environments and behavioral systems and the interrelationship of human behavior and environment; reports on research relating to evaluation and assessment of the effectiveness of environments designed to accomplish specific objectives; studies relating to the beliefs, meanings, values, and attitudes of individuals or groups concerning various environments; studies concerning physical environments whose human mission is not among their most salient characteristics, and physical environments whose human mission is largely implicit and/or socially undeveloped; studies of planning, policy, or political action aimed at controlling environment or behavior.
Typical Disciplines: Psychologists; environmentalists; planners; architects.
Intended Audience: College-educated public; graduate students; teachers; researchers; administrators; practitioners.
Special Features: Research reports; theoretical articles; book reviews; literature reviews; special theme for some issues; abstract for each article; annual index; advertising accepted.

Acceptance/Rejection Procedures: Each appropriate MS is sent to 2 members of the journal's editorial advisory board. Judgments are pooled by the editor, who makes the final decision.

Manuscript Disposition: Receipt of MS acknowledged; 6-8 weeks required for decision; "blind" refereeing; rejected MS returned; critique to author; 25-30% submitted MSS accepted; 25-30 MSS published/yr.; 6-9 months from acceptance to publication; first accepted, first published, except for special issues.

Style Requirements: Available upon request from editor or publisher; preferred length 25-30 pages, double spaced; 2 copies of MS; abstract required.

Payment: None to or by author for publication.

Reprints: 24 free; charge for additional depends on article length.

48 EVALUATION (1972) A Forum for Human Service Decision Makers

Laurence Kivens, Minneapolis Medical Research Foundation, 501 Park Ave. South, Minneapolis, MN 55415

Publisher: Minneapolis Medical Research Foundation, Inc.

Subscriptions: Not yet determined. Irregular, approximately twice yearly. Ca. 10,000. 80 pages/issue.

Description: "Is designed to draw together information on evaluation activities from all the relevant human service fields, to enable those involved in such activities to communicate with each other, and to inform various publics of the presence and vitality of these activities."

Article Content: Research project descriptions (articles or summaries); policy statements; overviews of a field; theoretical concepts; case studies--all in program evaluation.

Typical Disciplines: Primarily mental health fields but also human services delivery fields--public health, rehabilitation, geriatrics, criminal justice, education; and research and administration of program evaluation in all such fields.

Intended Audience: Intended to reach the entire range of persons interested in and engaged in evaluation, whether of individuals, groups, programs, organizations, or larger systems. It is oriented toward those who wish to understand better how to proceed with evaluation efforts and also how to deal with the consequences of such efforts; speaks to the theoretician and researcher, practitioner, administrator, manager, knowledgeable consumers and the informed public.

Special Features: Research reports; theoretical articles; book reviews; letters to the editor; editorials; brief summaries of research projects in program evaluation with address for obtaining more complete information.

Acceptance/Rejection Criteria: Editors encourage concise, substantive, useful, and original contributions in any of the following areas: new applications or sound reapplications of evaluation approaches; issues, problems, and successes related to past, present, or proposed evaluation efforts; changes in various programs as a result of the effects, intended or not, of evaluation efforts; and ways in which the skills of managers, researchers, and technical specialists have been used to develop evaluation designs.

Acceptance/Rejection Procedures: Review by minimum of two experts.

Manuscript Disposition: Receipt of MS acknowledged; 2-6 months required for decision; critique to author (usually); 20% submitted MSS accepted; 30 MSS published/yr.; 6-7 months from acceptance to publication; usually first accepted, first published.

Style Requirements: Guidelines available from Evaluation; maximum length 20 pages, double spaced.   Short summaries (from 100-1000 words) are also welcomed, provided they are directed to the point of program evaluation or increasing program effectiveness.   These need include only the name and location of the program, the methodology developed and/or used, possible applications and any available findings.   One copy of MS; no abstract.

Payment: None to or by author.

Reprints: Ten copies of magazine in which article appeared sent free; reprints available by request and at expense of requester.

49   HARVARD EDUCATIONAL REVIEW

Editorial Address: Editorial Office, Longfellow Hall, 13 Appian Way, Cambridge, MA   02138

Copyright: President and Fellows of Harvard College

Subscriptions: $12/yr., $18/2 yrs.   Available from Subscriber Service Dept., Longfellow Hall, 13 Appian Way, Cambridge, MA.   Quarterly.   125 pages/issue.

Description: "Journal of opinion and research in the field of education."

<u>Intended Audience</u>: Teachers; scholars; research workers in education; persons working in related fields.
<u>Special Features</u>: Book reviews; special theme for some issues; abstract for each article; advertising; notes on contributors; essay reviews; correspondence.

<u>Acceptance/Rejection Procedures</u>: Articles selected, edited, and published by an Editorial Board of graduate students at Harvard University. Discussion, disposition, and solicitation of MSS is the responsibility of the Editorial Board as a whole.
<u>Style Requirements</u>: 2 or more copies of MS; abstract required with MS; identify the author only on title page.

50 HIGHER EDUCATION (1972)

Robert Berdahl (North America) Dept. of Higher Education, State University of New York, Foster Annex, Buffalo, NY 14214
<u>Publisher & Copyright</u>: Elsevier Scientific Publishing Company, P.O. Box 211, Amsterdam, the Netherlands.
<u>Subscriptions</u>: Consult publishers. Quarterly. 132 pages/issue.

<u>Description</u>: "An international journal of higher education and educational planning. Purpose is to develop a forum for discussion based on contributions from different countries and different academic disciplines."
<u>Article Content</u>: Original articles--need not be comparative, but should keep international audience in mind; reports of significant innovations, experiments and developments; information with special reference to current developments.
<u>Typical Disciplines</u>: Interdisciplinary--education, philosophy, history, politics, psychology, sociology, economics.
<u>Intended Audience</u>: Legislators; government officials; those involved in policy decisions; teachers in all branches of higher education.
<u>Special Features</u>: Special theme some issues; book reviews; contributions on educational planning; advertising.

<u>Acceptance/Rejection Criteria</u>: Original articles, reports, information and book reviews on all aspects of higher (tertiary) education welcomed. Accounts written entirely within context of one culture, but keeping an international readership in mind, accepted. Whatever discipline or area of experience, if you have something significant to

write about post-secondary or tertiary education, you are
invited to contribute.

Style Requirements: Consult journal; style should be simple,
direct, and as non-technical as possible; double space
MS and leave wide margins; abstract of not more than
250 words required; abstract, list of symbols, references,
and tables should be on separate sheets.

Reprints: 50 free.

Special Note: Submit MSS on educational planning to Gareth
Williams, Department of Educational Research, University of Lancaster, Lancaster, England.

51 IMPROVING COLLEGE AND UNIVERSITY TEACHING
(1953)

Delmer M. Goode, Oregon State University, 101 Waldo Hall,
Corvallis, OR 97331

Publisher: Oregon State University Press, P. O. Box 689

Subscriptions: $6/yr, $9/two yrs., $12/three yrs. After
Jan. 1, 1975 $9/yr., $15/two yrs., $20/three yrs.
Quarterly. Ca. 3000. 80 pages/issue.

Description: "An international journal printing articles on
college and university teaching written by college or university teachers or students. Faculty members share
their teaching and professional experiences and their research for further classroom effectiveness."

Intended Audience: Presidents; deans; department heads;
faculty; students.

Special Features: Research reports; theoretical articles;
book reviews; editorials; special theme each issue; annual index; cumulative index for first ten years; limited
advertising.

Acceptance/Rejection Criteria: Policy is "open door." Any
sincere MS is acceptable. Printing production limitations, however, impose serious problems.

Manuscript Disposition: Receipt of MS acknowledged; 3-5
months required for decision; 125 MSS published/yr.

Style Requirements: Preferred length 1600 words; 1 copy of
MS; no abstract.

Payment: None to or by author.

Reprints: Available at charge.

52 IMPETUS MAGAZINE (1972)

Clarke B. Fine, P. O. Box 1021, Redlands, CA 92373
Publisher: Clarke B. Fine
Institutional Affiliation: Johnston College, Redlands, CA
Subscriptions: Instit. & Indiv. $2.98/yr. Available from
P. O. Box 1021, Redlands, CA. Issued 4 times/yr.
Ca. 5000. 32 pages/issue.

Description: "Magazine exploring alternatives in today's education. About alternatives in experimental education, new
programs (innovative ones) and Johnston College. "
Article Content: Anything that relates in any way to alternative higher education or alternative programs in "traditional" schools.
Intended Audience: Teachers; researchers; administrators;
practitioners; students--people related to higher education.
Special Features: Research reports; theoretical articles; letters to the editor; new or innovative programs.

Acceptance/Rejection Criteria: All articles must be related
in some way to experimental and/or alternative higher
education. Preference is given to articles about new,
innovative programs at work on campuses and special research projects.
Acceptance/Rejection Procedures: All MSS go to an editorial
board composed of faculty members, journalism professors and students at Johnston College, Redlands. The
board reviews each article then votes on which to publish.
Manuscript Disposition: Receipt of MS acknowledged; 30 days
required for decision; rejected MS returned (all photos
returned with MS); 85% submitted MSS accepted; 20 MSS
published/yr.; 3 to 5 months from acceptance to publication; first accepted, first published.
Style Requirements: Write to Impetus; preferred length 8 to
10 pages, double spaced; minimum length 8 pages, maximum 20 pages; 2 copies of MS; no abstract.
Payment: No charge to authors except possible costs for film
if photos are needed; no payment to authors except in
commissioned articles.
Reprints: 20 free; $35/1000 for additional.

53 INSTRUCTIONAL SCIENCE (1972)

Roulette Wm. Smith, Instructional Science, Phelps Hall, University of California, Santa Barbara, CA 93106 (for
Americas).

Publisher: Elsevier Publishing Co., P.O. Box 211, Amsterdam, the Netherlands.
Subscriptions: Consult publisher (approximately $16.67). Quarterly.

Description: "Purpose of journal is to deal with instructional science on a broad interdisciplinary level and in greater depth than normally found."
Article Content: "Instruction" interpreted very literally to cover almost the whole gamut of processes by which people self-consciously seek to make themselves understood to others. Instruction is thought of as related to purposive communication. Also concerned with all aspects of learning, especially with the conditions under which teaching or training succeeds or fails.
Typical Disciplines: Broad, interdisciplinary.
Special Features: Research Reports; theoretical articles; book reviews; letters to the editor; literature reviews; advertising.

Acceptance/Rejection Criteria: Preference to articles constituting significant contributions to science of instruction; articles having few theoretical or practical consequences discouraged; authoritative review articles, reports of significant new work, and theoretical papers of an original or controversial kind are especially welcome; exclude technical articles on animal behavior and biochemical mechanisms of learning unless relevance to human instruction is demonstrated; all articles must be self-contained (intelligible without requiring extensive research); scholarly articles on learning and related subjects also welcome.
Style Requirements: All MSS except reviews should say what contributions are being made to the theory or practice of instructional science, and this statement should be clearly incorporated in the abstract and summary as well as in the main text; longer articles of 8000 words or more welcomed; 12,000 words maximum length except in exceptional cases; abstract required; style requirements available from editor or publisher; contact with one of the Editors at an early stage, before final preparation of the MS, is appreciated.
Reprints: 50 preprints free to senior author; additional available at charge.

54 INTELLECT (1915)
   formerly School & Society

William W. Brickman, Editor, Intellect, Graduate School of
   Education, University of Pennsylvania, Philadelphia, PA
   19174
Publisher: Stanley Lehrer
Organizational Affiliation of Journal: Society for the Advance-
   ment of Education
Subscriptions: Instit. & Indiv. $15/yr. Indiv. member
   $10/yr. Available from Intellect, 1860 Broadway, New
   York, N.Y. 10023. Monthly, October-May. Ca. 9500.
   68 pages/issue.

Description: "To present articles and other writings on historical and contemporary issues and problems in education, society, international relations, the humanities, and
   related fields for a readership of scholars, professionals,
   and interested laity. Broad international level."
Article Content: Education; current affairs; social problems;
   college and university enrollments in America; reforming
   teacher education; educational strategies for building new
   societies; alternative school systems; faculty unionization.
Typical Disciplines: Education; sociology; political science;
   humanities; international relations.
Intended Audience: College and university faculty members
   and administrators; nationally notable thinkers; researchers; students; those in above disciplines.
Special Features: Research reports; theoretical articles; letters to the editor; editorials; literature reviews; abstract
   for each article; annual index; national report section;
   notable book selections; advertising.

Acceptance/Rejection Criteria: Scholarship; originality; readability; critical analysis.
Manuscript Disposition: One month required for decision;
   rejected MS returned (if postage accompanies MS); 15%
   submitted MSS accepted; 150 MSS published/yr.; 6 months
   from acceptance to publication.
Style Requirements: Request statement from editor; preferred
   length 3500 words; minimum length 1000 words, maximum
   5000; 1 copy of MS; abstract of 1 sentence required.
Payment: None to or by author.
Reprints: Available for charge.

55 INTERCHANGE (1970) A Journal of Educational Studies
formerly Ontario Journal of Educational Research

Dr. Andrew Effrat, The Ontario Institute for Studies in Education, 252 Bloor Street West, Toronto, Ontario M5S IV6, Canada
Publisher & Copyright: The Ontario Institute for Studies in Education
Subscriptions: Instit. $10/yr. Indiv. $7/yr. Student $5/yr. Quarterly. Ca. 2000. 112-128 pages/issue.

Description: "Interchange is an international and interdisciplinary journal of educational studies. It emphasizes the articulation of theory with empirical research, encourages confrontations between competing perspectives and methodologies, and the development of practitioner-oriented policy statements."
Article Content: Broad range from de-schooling society to multivariate techniques for educational research.
Typical Disciplines: Any with a specialty in education, such as psychology, sociology, history.
Intended Audience: School trustees, administrators; teachers in public school; members of government departments; researchers; students.
Special Features: Research reports; theoretical articles; book reviews; hortatory or polemical articles; literature reviews; abstract for each article; annual index; advertising.

Acceptance/Rejection Criteria: Importance and originality of contribution to educational theory and research adequacy of argument, methods and review of the literature; validity of conclusions; relevance of its argument for practical questions or its implications for educational or social change.
Acceptance/Rejection Procedures: After the MS has been read by at least 2 outside readers, the staff discusses it in some detail and rejects, accepts with revisions suggested, or accepts.
Manuscript Disposition: Receipt of MS acknowledged; 6-8 weeks from acceptance to decision; "blind" refereeing; rejected MS returned; critique to author; 15% submitted MSS accepted; 40 MSS published/yr.; 6 months from acceptance to publication; first accepted, first published.
Style Requirements: APA Publication Manual; preferred length 30 pages, double spaced; 3 copies of MS; abstract required.
Payment: None to or by author.
Reprints: 10 free; $1.00 additional for each reprint.

56 JOURNAL OF ABNORMAL PSYCHOLOGY

Leonard D. Eron, Department of Psychology, Box 4348, University of Illinois at Chicago Circle, Chicago, IL 60680
Publisher & Copyright: American Psychological Association, Inc., 1200 Seventeenth Street, N.W., Washington, D.C. 20036
Subscriptions: $24/yr. Available on calendar-year basis only. Bimonthly. Ca. 5000.

Description: "Devoted to basic research and theory in the broad field of abnormal behavior, its determinants, and its correlates."
Article Content: Psychopathology--its development, treatment or remission, and its symptomatology and course; normal processes in abnormal individuals; pathological or atypical features of the behavior of normal persons; experimental studies, with human or animal subjects, relating to emotional behavior or pathology; social or group effects on adjustment and pathological processes; tests of hypotheses from psychoanalytic or other psychological theory.

Acceptance/Rejection Criteria: Case histories, experiments on hypnosis, theoretical papers of scholarly substance on personality or emotional abnormality, studies of therapy and behavior change, experimental studies and analysis of abnormal behavior and motivation, studies of patient populations--all fall within scope of the journal.
Style Requirements: APA Publication Manual; 3 copies of MS; abstract of 100-120 words required, should conform to style of Psychological Abstracts; journal does not use abbreviations.
Reprints: When authors receive galley proofs of their articles, they may order reprints from the printer.

57 JOURNAL OF APPLIED BEHAVIOR ANALYSIS (1968)

Dr. Steward Agras, Department of Psychiatry, Stanford University School of Medicine, Stanford, CA 94305
Publisher & Copyright: Society for the Experimental Analysis of Behavior, Inc.
Subscriptions: Instit. $18/yr. Indiv. $10/yr. Student $6/yr. Available from Mary Louise Sherman, Business Manager, Dept. of Human Development, University of Kansas, Lawrence, KS 66044. Quarterly. Ca. 6850. 180 pages/issue.

Description: "Primarily for the original publication of reports of experimental research involving applications of the experimental analysis of behavior to problems of social importance. It will also publish technical articles relevant to such research and discussions of issues arising from behavioral applications."

Article Content: Behavior modification; experimental demonstrations of effective therapeutic, educational, and social engineering procedures.

Typical Disciplines: Psychology; sociology; social work; education; special education; speech; criminology; law.

Special Features: Research reports; literature reviews; abstract of each article; annual index; advertising.

Acceptance/Rejection Procedures: MS assigned to 1 of 7 associate editors; then assigned (by assoc. editor) to 3 or 4 reviewers; reviewers' comments on MS are read by assoc. ed., who then sends decision of accept/reject and copies of reviewers' comments to author.

Manuscript Disposition: Receipt of MS acknowledged; 10 weeks from receipt of MS to decision; rejected MS returned; critique to author; 27% submitted MSS accepted; 80 MSS published/yr.; 6 months from acceptance to publication; first accepted, first published.

Style Requirements: Consult journal, also Vol. 2 (1969) spring issue; preferred length 10-30 pages, double spaced; 5 copies of MS; abstract required.

Payment: None to or by author for publication.

Reprints: None free.

58 JOURNAL OF APPLIED BEHAVIORAL SCIENCE (1965)

Matthew B. Miles (Center for Policy Research) 94 Sparkill Ave., Tappan, N.Y. 10983

Publisher: NTL Institute

Subscriptions: $15/yr. Issued 6/yr. Ca. 7000. 128 pages/ issue, with one double issue yearly. Address all non-editorial matters to: Managing Editor, P.O. Box 9155 Rosslyn Station, Arlington, VA 22209

Description: "This journal is committed to the advancement of valid knowledge of the goals, processes, and outcomes of planned change and social innovation involving persons, groups, organizations, and larger systems."

Typical Disciplines: Psychology; sociology; business; therapy training; organization development; education.

Intended Audience: The behavioral scientist who cares about
    understanding how planned change works and what its ef-
    fects are; the thoughtful change agent, regardless of his/
    her formal credentials, who wants to develop a social
    practice based on knowledge; clients and system members
    who are involved in efforts at planned change and social
    innovation; students; administrators; teachers; researchers;
    practitioners.
Special Features: Research reports; theoretical articles; book
    reviews; letters to the editor; abstract for each article;
    "present shock"--analyses of pressing social needs with-
    out current application of behavioral science; case studies.

Acceptance/Rejection Criteria: Priority given to articles
    which (1) develop and test new theories and concepts of
    change which have predictive and explanatory power and
    clear implications for action; (2) examine new social
    institutions, social inventions and practices, and methods
    of intervention, in order to understand their processes
    and outcomes; (3) make direct, explicit analysis of the
    underlying values, implicit social models, categories and
    images, assumptions and biases which are always part
    and parcel of the theory and practice of planned change.
    Emphasis on careful empirical work--either quantitative
    or in the form of qualitative analyses and case studies--
    which illuminate the interplay among theory, practice,
    and values in the domain of planned change.   Empirical
    research and theoretical/practical discussion of change
    strategies of any sort; no limitations placed on the social
    problems and situation to which change efforts addressed;
    coherence, explicitness, self-awareness, replicability and
    liveliness desired.
Acceptance/Rejection Procedure: MSS judged by at least two
    members of the Editorial Board or panel of Consulting
    Editors.   Articles typically read "blind."
Manuscript Disposition: Receipt of MS acknowledged; 3-4
    months from receipt to decision; "blind" refereeing; re-
    jected MS returned; critique to author; 15% submitted
    MSS accepted; 40 MSS published/yr.; 14 months from
    acceptance to publication.
Style Requirements: Consult journal; articles normally run
    from 1500 to 7500 words (6 to 30 double spaced typewrit-
    ten pages, including figures, footnotes, tables, and refer-
    ences); 3 copies of MS; abstract of 100-150 words; all
    copy double spaced; MS should clearly indicate what parts
    the author played in the situations reported on.
Payment: None to author; author shares cost of extensive

graphic work.

Reprints: 3 complimentary copies of journal issue; offprints may be ordered at press time, reprints at any time (100 minimum).

59 JOURNAL OF APPLIED PSYCHOLOGY (1917)

Dr. Edwin A. Fleishman, American Institutes for Research, 8555 Sixteenth St., Silver Spring, MD 20910

Publisher & Copyright: American Psychological Association, 1200 17th St., N.W., Washington, D.C. 20036.

Subscriptions: $24/yr. Available on Jan.-Dec. basis only. Bimonthly. Ca. 4700. 135 pages/issue.

Description: "Devoted primarily to original investigations, contributing new knowledge and understanding to any field of applied psychology, except clinical psychology. A theoretical or review article may be accepted if it represents a special contribution to an applied field."

Article Content: Job satisfaction; motivation; human performance; test development; group processes; consumer psychology; educational measurement; organizational psychology; training; management; information processing.

Intended Audience: Psychologists doing research or working in such settings as business, industry, government, police and correctional systems, transportation and defense systems, space and other new environments, educational systems, urban affairs, health systems and institutions, and consumer affairs. Also psychologists teaching at all academic levels.

Special Features: Research reports; theoretical articles; abstract for each issue; cumulative index; available on microform; advertising.

Acceptance/Rejection Criteria: Significance in contributing new knowledge to the field; technical adequacy; appropriateness for journal; clarity of presentation; conciseness and respect for reader time; unambiguous and simple vocabulary with technical and erudite words used only when simpler ones inadequate; conformity to accepted technical style in tables, terminology, and references; conclusions that are clearly related to the evidence presented.

Acceptance/Rejection Procedures: Blind reviewing may be obtained if specifically requested at the time a MS is submitted. In such cases, author's name and affiliation should appear only on a separate title page.

Manuscript Disposition: Receipt of MS acknowledged; 2-3 months required for decision; rejected MS returned; critique to author; 24% submitted MSS accepted; 110 MSS published/yr.; 10 to 12 months from acceptance to publication; first accepted, first published.

Style Requirements: APA Publication Manual and journal; check several recent issues to get idea of length of MS; 3 copies of MS (one original); abstract of 100-120 words required; all copy must be double spaced.

Payment: None to or by author.

Reprints: None free. Order from printer prior to publication.

60 JOURNAL OF APPLIED SOCIAL PSYCHOLOGY (1971)

Dr. Siegfried Streufert, Psychological Sciences, Purdue University, Lafayette, IN 47907

Publisher: V. H. Winston & Sons, Inc., 1511 K Street, N.W., Washington, D.C. 20005. Copyright: Scripta Publishing Corporation.

Subscriptions: Instit. $30/yr. Indiv. $16/yr. Quarterly. Ca. 1000. 120 pages/issue.

Description: "Will disseminate findings from behavioral science research which have applications to current problems of society. Intends to bridge the theoretical and applied areas of social research. Serves as a means of communication among scientists, as well as between researchers and those engaged in the task of solving social problems."

Article Content: Attitudes and attitude change; perception; personality variables; negotiation and bargaining; crowding & pollution; elections & politics; environmental & social ecology; family planning; modification of behavior; racial and sexual discrimination; training and education.

Typical Disciplines: Psychology; sociology; behavioral political science; education.

Intended Audience: College-educated public; students; teachers; researchers; administrators; practitioners.

Special Features: Research reports; theoretical articles; editorials; abstract for each article; annual index.

Acceptance/Rejection Criteria: Preference given to MSS reporting laboratory and field research in primarily three areas: problems of society; problems of human development, learning, and education; and problems of political, social, and industrial organizations. Tentative suggestions for application of research findings should be included. Theoretical papers are acceptable in limited numbers, and should include some research data whenever possible. Reviews of pertinent literature should be made with applicability in mind.

Manuscript Disposition: Receipt of MS acknowledged; 6 weeks to 2 months from receipt to acceptance; rejected MS returned; critique to author; 14% submitted MSS accepted; 40 MSS published/yr.; accepted MSS published in next issue (no delay); first accepted, first published.

Style Requirements: APA Publication Manual; maximum length 35 pages, double spaced; 2 copies of MS; abstract required.

Payment: None to or by author.

Reprints: Charge depends on length of MS.

61 JOURNAL OF CLINICAL PSYCHOLOGY (1945)

F. C. Thorne, 4 Conant Square, Brandon, VT 05733

Publisher & Copyright: Clinical Psychology Publishing Co., Inc., 4 Conant Square.

Subscriptions: Instit. & Indiv. $20/yr. APA members & students $15/yr. Quarterly. Ca. 2500. 125 pages/issue.

Description: "Purpose of this journal is to provide the most comprehensive coverage of research and practice in the field of clinical psychology in a concise, readable form."

Article Content: Clinical judgment and diagnostic methods; psychopathology and psychodynamics; psychodiagnosis; objective tests of ability; psychodiagnosis: objective personality inventories and rating scales; psychodiagnosis: projective methods; psychotherapeutic processes.

Typical Disciplines: Psychology and psychiatry.

Intended Audience: Advanced graduate students & specialists; researchers; practitioners.

Special Features: Research reports; editorial opinions; annual index; occasional monographs bound in at no extra cost.

Acceptance/Rejection Procedures: Major decisions are made by Editor with occasional consideration by Editorial Board or other referees.

Manuscript Disposition: Receipt of MS acknowledged; research reports only accepted; two weeks from receipt to decision; rejected MS returned; critique to author; 60% submitted MSS accepted; 120 MSS published/yr.; six months from acceptance to publication; first accepted, first published.

Style Requirements: Statement available from publisher; preferred length 5-6 pages, double spaced; minimum length 2 pages, maximum 8 pages; 3 copies of MS; summary required with MS.

Payment: None to author; author is assessed a page charge which is determined by the editor and based on length and amount of special composition.

Reprints: Available at charge.

JOURNAL OF COMMUNITY PSYCHOLOGY

Special Note: Beginning in January 1973 the JOURNAL OF CLINICAL PSYCHOLOGY was published in two sections. Section I continues to be known as the JOURNAL OF CLINICAL PSYCHOLOGY. Section II is known as the JOURNAL OF COMMUNITY PSYCHOLOGY. It offers to its readers a wide spectrum of papers dealing with the applications of psychology in community settings, and emphasizes solid research reports and program evaluations. Article Content and Special Features include: characteristics and evaluations of training programs for mental health professionals; drug addiction; treatment techniques; juvenile delinquency; assessment of interpersonal skills; criminal behavior; mental health services in a correctional mental hospital; abortion and its effects; personality assessment; limited studies in military psychology; evaluation and assessment studies of community psychology programs; periodic monograph supplements. Both these journals will be operated as a unit. Same subscription price for both ($20 each).

62 JOURNAL OF COLLEGE STUDENT PERSONNEL (1959)

Albert B. Hood, W112 East Hall, University of Iowa, Iowa City, IA 52242

Publisher & Copyright: American Personnel and Guidance Association, 1607 New Hampshire Ave. N.W., Washington, D.C. 20009

Subscriptions: Instit. $15/yr. Indiv. non-member $15/yr. Indiv. member $8/yr. Student member $4/yr. Bimonthly. Ca. 8000. 96 pages/issue.

Description: "The official journal of the American College
Personnel Association, a division of the APGA. Publishes
research, critical thought, literature reviews, and innovative ideas in the broad field of college counseling and
student personnel administration. "

Article Content: College counseling; admissions; financial aid;
environment; housing; vocational development; student
characteristics.

Intended Audience: Advanced graduate students; teachers; researchers; administrators; practitioners.

Special Features: Research reports; theoretical articles; editorials; literature reviews; abstract for each article; brief
descriptions of innovative practices; information & issues
sections; minutes of association meetings and association
news.

Acceptance/Rejection Criteria: Significance of MS; design of
research (if research report); technical adequacy; clarity
and conciseness of presentation; appropriateness for this
journal.

Acceptance/Rejection Procedures: Sent to two reviewers on
editorial board. Blind reviewing with editor having final
decision.

Manuscript Disposition: Receipt of MS acknowledged; 60 days
from receipt to decision; author nominates referees;
"blind" refereeing; rejected MS returned; critique to author; 35% submitted MSS accepted; 84 MSS published/yr.;
4-6 months from acceptance to publication; generally first
accepted, first published.

Style Requirements: APA Publication Manual; preferred length
8-12 pages, double spaced; minimum length 2 pages, maximum 14 pages; 2 copies of MS; abstract required.

Payment: None to or by author.

Reprints: 50 free; additional charge based on length of article, and available in lots of 50.

63 JOURNAL OF CONSULTING AND CLINICAL PSYCHOLOGY
(1937)

Brendan A. Maher, 1120 William James Hall, Harvard University, 33 Kirkland Street, Cambridge, MA 02138

Publisher & Copyright: American Psychological Association,
1200 17th Street, N.W., Washington, D.C. 20036

Subscriptions: Instit. & Indiv. $24/yr. Available on Jan.-
Dec. basis only. Bimonthly. Ca. 6800. 170 pages/is-
sue.

Description: "Publishes original contributions on the following topics: the development, validity, and use of techniques of diagnosis and treatment in disordered behavior;
studies of populations of clinical interest, such as hospital and prison samples; cross-cultural and demographic
studies of interest for the behavior disorders; studies of
personality and of its assessment and development where
these have a clear bearing on problems of consulting and
clinical psychology; the etiology and characteristics of
psychopathological states; case studies pertinent to the
preceding topics; papers of a theoretical nature considered
within space limitations."

Article Content: Community psychology; psychotherapy, behavior modification, life history research; schizophrenia,
psychopathy; intellectual and cognitive disorders; personality assessment; psychomatic disorders.

Typical Disciplines: Psychology--clinical; psychiatry; social
work; educators.

Intended Audience: Teachers; researchers; administrators;
practitioners; students in psychology and education.

Special Features: Case reports; some theoretical articles;
literature reviews; brief reports; abstract for each article; annual index starting 1974 (previously separate bi-
annual indexes); advertising.

Acceptance/Rejection Criteria: Appropriateness to journal;
significance of contribution to clinical/consulting psychology; adequacy & clarity of communication; adherence to
APA publication standards.

Acceptance/Rejection Procedures: MS sent to one or more
editorial consultants for reviews; if reviews strong, documented, MS dealt with as recommended; if reviews un-
clear or scanty, additional reviews found. Alternate
journals suggested for re-submission of inappropriate MS.

Manuscript Disposition: Receipt of MS acknowledged; 10-12
weeks required for decision; rejected MS returned; critique to author; 20% submitted MSS accepted; 180 MSS
published/yr.; 6 months from acceptance to publication;
first accepted, first published.

Style Requirements: APA Publication Manual and journal;
length requirements not applicable except for Brief Report where 3 typed pages is maximum; 3 copies of MS;
abstract required.

Payment: None to author; changes in galleys constitute charge
for author.

Reprints: None free; may be ordered for payment, when galley proofs checked by author.

64 JOURNAL OF COUNSELING PSYCHOLOGY (1954)

[A new editor took over in the fall of 1974; name unknown as
of press time.]
Publisher & Copyright: American Psychological Association,
1200 17th Street, N.W., Washington, D.C. 20036
Subscriptions: $15/yr. Available on a Jan.-Dec. basis only.
Bimonthly. Ca. 6100. 100 pages/issue.

Description: "To publish MSS related to research, theory,
and practice directly related to counseling psychology.
Topical reviews of research and other systematic surveys
may be included periodically as well as measurement
studies which directly relate to counseling."
Intended Audience: Psychologists and counselors in schools,
colleges and universities, public and private agencies,
business, industry, and military agencies; students in
psychology and education.
Special Features: Research reports; theoretical articles; abstract for each article; annual and cumulative index; advertising.

Acceptance/Rejection Criteria: Conciseness and respect for
reader time; unambiguous, simple vocabulary; conformity
to accepted technical style in tables, figures, etc.; conclusions clearly related to evidence presented.
Acceptance/Rejection Procedures: The MS is received by
the editor who assigns and sends it to a consulting editor
who reads and comments on it. The consultant returns
it to the editor who decides concerning acceptance and a
letter is sent to the author notifying him of the decision.
Manuscript Disposition: Receipt of MS acknowledged; 6 weeks
required for decision; "blind" refereeing; rejected MS returned; critique to author; 35% submitted MSS accepted;
6 months from acceptance to publication; generally first
MSS accepted are first published.
Style Requirements: APA Publication Manual; preferred length
15 pages, double spaced; 2 copies of MS; abstract required.
Payment: None to or by author.
Reprints: Available at charge.

65 JOURNAL OF CROSS-CULTURAL PSYCHOLOGY (1970)

Walter J. Lonner, Center for Cross-Cultural Research, Department of Psychology, Western Washington State College,
Bellingham, WA 98225

Publisher & Copyright: Sage Publications, Inc., 275 So.
Beverly Drive, Beverly Hills, CA 90212
Organizational Affiliation: International Association for Cross-
Cultural Psychology and Western Washington State College.
Subscriptions: Instit. $18/yr. Professionals & teachers,
$10/yr. Student $9/yr. Quarterly. Ca. 1000+. 128
pages/issue.

Description: "Publishes empirical research and occasional
speculative or theoretical papers in cross-cultural psychology, psychological anthropology, and cross-cultural
aspects of other behavioral sciences."
Article Content: Intelligence; perception; psychopathology;
motivation; personality; cognition; psycholinguistics; attitudes; social behavior.
Typical Disciplines: While JCCP is broadly a psychological
journal, the closely related disciplines of anthropology,
sociology, criminology, psychiatry, psycholinguistics,
personnel and management and the behavioral aspects of
political science are represented.
Intended Audience: Researchers; teachers; practitioners;
students.
Special Features: Research reports; theoretical articles;
book reviews; editorials; abstract for each article; brief
sketches of authors; annual index; when desirable and possible, longer papers will appear in monograph form.

Acceptance/Rejection Criteria: Will publish exclusively cross-
cultural behavioral and social research. Cross-cultural
studies concentrating on psychological phenomena as they
are conditioned by cultures or subcultures, as well as
other social and behavioral research which focuses on
the individual as a member of the cultural group, rather
than on the macroscopic group, are preferred. Comparative correlational & experimental inferential research,
rather than descriptive or speculative observations, as
well as theoretical & critical papers will be considered.
The relevance of the research for cross-cultural comparisons of psychological variables must be clear.
Acceptance/Rejection Procedures: Each appropriate MS is
sent to two members of the Editorial Advisory Board.
These judgments are pooled and are used by the editor
in making final decisions. Review rating sheet used.
Manuscript Disposition: Receipt of MS acknowledged; 5 to 7
weeks required for decision; "blind" refereeing; rejected
MS returned; critique to author; 25% (and declining) submitted MSS accepted; 40 MSS published/yr.; 6 to 9

months from acceptance to publication; usually first accepted, first published.

Style Requirements: Consult journal; preferred length 15-20 pages, double spaced; minimum length 5 pages, maximum 40 pages; 3 copies of MS; abstract required.

Payment: None to or by author for publication.

Reprints: 25 free; additional at nominal charge.

66 JOURNAL OF EDUCATION (owned by Boston U since 1953)

Editor, Boston University Journal of Education, School of Education, 765 Commonwealth Avenue, Boston, MA 02215

Publisher & Copyright: Boston University, Journal of Education

Subscriptions: Instit. & Indiv. $5/yr. Quarterly.

Description: "Dedicated to the continuing development of educators and students, to the encouragement of interest and participation in research and theory and their application in the field, and to the reflection of an ever-increasing awareness of the impact of education on humanity. Serves as a forum for the presentation of viable issues and concerns in education."

Typical Disciplines: Education; psychology; educational philosophy.

Intended Audience: Students and educators in public schools, private schools, junior colleges, universities, industry and government.

Special Features: Research reports; theoretical articles; book reviews; letters to the editor; available on microform.

Acceptance/Rejection Criteria: Relevance; generalizability; clarity of expression.

Manuscript Disposition: Receipt of MS acknowledged; 6 weeks required for decision; "blind" refereeing; rejected MS returned; critique to author; 15-25% submitted MSS accepted.

Style Requirements: APA Publication Manual; no minimum or maximum length for articles; 3 copies of MS (original and 2 copies); abstract of 100-200 words; for unsolicited articles the author's name and address must be on a separate page from the MS proper to facilitate blind referee system; double space.

Payment: None to or by author.

Reprints: Rate of approximately $1.25 per copy plus postage.

67 THE JOURNAL OF EDUCATION OF THE FACULTY OF
EDUCATION (1957)

L. F. Ashley, Faculty of Education, University of British
Columbia, Vancouver, B. C. , Canada
Publisher & Copyright: The University of B. C.
Subscriptions: $1. 25/yr. Annual. Ca. 1500. 100 pages/
issue.

Description: "Examines selected topics in education, frequently in special issues with a particular theme. "
Article Content: Educational history; values of education;
adult education.
Intended Audience: Faculty; researchers; administrators;
practitioners; students.
Special Features: Research reports; theoretical articles;
special theme each issue.

Acceptance/Rejection Criteria: Scholarly research; readable
style; topic of fairly wide educational interest.
Acceptance/Rejection Procedures: MSS for the most part
commissioned by special issue editors. Unsolicited MSS
read by several scholars in field and accepted or returned.
Manuscript Disposition: Receipt of MS acknowledged; rejected
MS returned; 50% submitted MSS accepted; 10 MSS pub-
lished/yr. ; one year from acceptance to publication.
Style Requirements: Turabian; preferred length 16-20 pages,
double spaced; minimum 5-10 pages, maximum 25-30
pages; 1 copy of MS; no abstract.
Payment: None to or by author.
Reprints: Not available.

68 JOURNAL OF EDUCATIONAL DATA PROCESSING (1963)

Sally Douglas, Cabrillo College, 6500 Soquel Drive, Aptos,
CA 95003
Publisher & Copyright: Educational Systems Corporation
Subscriptions: $11/yr. Available from Mrs. Anne Tondow,
P. O. Box 2995, Stanford, CA 94305. Bimonthly. Ca.
1500. 30 pages/issue. (Make checks payable to Educa-
tional Systems Corp.)

Description: "Devoted primarily to the publication of technical information, original research, and descriptions of
the organization and operation of data-processing systems
in education. "

Article Content: Applications of data processing in educational administration (scheduling, attendance, accounting); data processing curriculum; utilization of computers as a means of instruction.

Intended Audience: Administrators of data processing services in educational institutions; teachers of data processing; schools of education--students and teachers; researchers.

Special Features: Research reports; theoretical articles; book reviews; special theme for some issues; annual and cumulative index; review of recent technological developments; available on microform.

Acceptance/Rejection Criteria: Articles must be well-written, timely, and an in-depth discussion of some aspect of the specialized field of educational data processing.

Acceptance/Rejection Procedures: MSS are submitted to the editor who reviews and determines the eligibility of each article.

Manuscript Disposition: Receipt of MS acknowledged; 2-3 months required for decision; rejected MS returned; critique to author; 80% submitted MSS accepted; 15 MSS published/yr.; 2-3 months from acceptance to publication; first accepted, first published.

Style Requirements: Consult journal and APA Publication Manual; preferred length 20 pages, double spaced; minimum length 7 pages, maximum 30 pages; 2 copies of MS (including original); no abstract.

Payment: None to or by author.

Reprints: 5 free copies; additional reprints may be ordered before press run or after the press, according to two price schedules.

69 JOURNAL OF EDUCATIONAL MEASUREMENT (1964)

Robert L. Linn, Department of Educational Psychology, Education Building, University of Illinois, Urbana, IL 61801

Publisher & Copyright: National Council of Measurement in Education

Subscriptions: Instit. & Indiv. $10/yr. Quarterly. Ca. 2200. 80 pages/issue. Address business correspondence to: NCME Secretary-Treasurer Irvin J. Lehmann, Office of Evaluation Service, Michigan State University, East Lansing, MI 48823

Description: "Publishes original measurement research and

reports of applications of measurement in an educational
context. "
Intended Audience: Educational researchers; school psychologists; tests and measurement specialists; students; those
concerned with applied problems in educational measurement.
Special Features: Research reports; solicited book reviews;
solicited reviews of current standardized educational and
psychological tests and of other important measurement
works; abstract for each article; advertising.

Acceptance/Rejection Criteria: Deal with significant problems
in educational measurement; advance state of knowledge
in some generalizable way; clearly written, as concise
as possible; empirical studies appropriately designed and
executed. Low probability of acceptance to: technical
papers better suited to, say, Psychometrika; reports of
routine studies in which the psychometric properties of
a single test have been investigated; traditional prediction
studies in which the academic success in a particular institution is the criterion; studies more concerned with the
development of concepts or theories in some discipline
than with the implications for educational measurement.
Acceptance/Rejection Procedures: MSS sent with authors'
names depleted to qualified reviewers. Editor makes
final decision.
Manuscript Disposition: 2 months required for decision;
"blind" refereeing; rejected MS returned; critique to
author; 20% submitted MSS accepted; 35 MSS published/
yr.; 9 months from acceptance to publication; first accepted, first published; authors desiring an acknowledg-
ment of the receipt of their MS should include a stamped,
self-addressed postcard for this purpose.
Style Requirements: APA Publication Manual, journal; preferred length 15 pages, double spaced; 3 copies of MS;
abstract of no more than 150 words.
Payment: None to or by author.
Reprints: 50; additional ordered with galley proofs.

70 JOURNAL OF EDUCATIONAL PSYCHOLOGY

Joanna Williams, P.O. Box 51, Teachers College, Columbia
University, New York, NY 10027
Publisher & Copyright: American Psychological Association,
1200 17th Street, N.W., Washington, D.C. 20036
Subscriptions: Instit. & Indiv. $24/yr. Available on calendar

year (Jan.-Dec.) basis only. Bimonthly. 166 pages/ issue. Ca. 5200.

Description: "Publishes original investigations and theoretical papers dealing with problems of learning and teaching and with the psychological development, relationships, and adjustment of the individual. Journal articles pertain to all levels of education and to all age groups."

Intended Audience: Undergraduate and graduate students in education and psychology; researchers; people in educational psychology.

Special Features: Research reports; theoretical articles; abstract for each article; annual index; advertising.

Acceptance/Rejection Criteria: Preference is given to studies of the more complex types of behavior, especially in or relating to educational settings.

Manuscript Disposition: Receipt of MS acknowledged; 2 months required for decision; "blind" refereeing; rejected MS returned; critique to author; 1 year from acceptance to publication; first published, first accepted.

Style Requirements: APA Publication Manual, journal; preferred length 15 pages; all copy double spaced; two copies of MS, one the original; include with each copy of the MS a cover sheet showing title, name of author, institutional affiliation, date submitted; for blind refereeing the MS itself should not identify author; first page of MS should include title and date; abstract of 100-120 words required.

Payment: None to or by author for publication.

Reprints: Order from printer when receive galley proofs.

71 JOURNAL OF EDUCATIONAL RESEARCH (1920)

Wilson Thiede (University of Wisconsin) Box 1605, Madison, WI 53701

Publisher & Copyright: Dembar Educational Research Services, Inc., Box 1605, Madison, WI 53701

Subscriptions: Instit. & Indiv. $10/yr. Student $7.50/yr. Issued 10/yr. Ca. 6200. 48 pages/issue.

Description: "Publishes research articles and critiques designed to advance the scientific study of education and improve field practice."

Intended Audience: General public; students in education; teachers; researchers; administrators; practitioners.

Special Features: Research reports; book reviews; literature
  reviews; special theme each issue; editorials; research
  briefs; abstract for each article; annual index; available
  on microform; advertising.

Acceptance/Rejection Criteria: Articles should generally possess certain elements including a statement of the problem;
  related research (minimal and highly selective); population
  and methodology; presentation of data; findings and conclusions; implications for practice; summarizing statement.
  Also seek simplicity and clarity.
Manuscript Disposition: Receipt of MS acknowledged; 2 months
  required for decision; "blind" refereeing; rejected MS returned; critique to author; 25% submitted MSS accepted;
  80-100 MSS published/yr.; 9-12 months from acceptance
  to publication; first accepted, first published.
Style Requirements: Consult journal or request guidelines
  from editorial office; articles usually relatively short,
  from 1500 to 3000 words; double space; two copies of
  MS; abstract of not more than 120 words; in a research
  paper abstract should include statements of the problem,
  the method, the data, and the conclusions; for review or
  discussion article, abstract should state the topics covered and the central thesis(es). Journal follows A Manual of Style, University of Chicago.
Payment: None to author; publisher charges a contributor's
  fee of approximately $6 per printed page of about 1,200
  words, billed upon publication. Authors are charged for
  changes in tables, figures, or copy made when article is
  in galley form.
Reprints: 10 complimentary copies of journal issue; reprints
  charged at cost.

72 JOURNAL OF THE EXPERIMENTAL ANALYSIS OF BE-
  HAVIOR (1958)

Victor G. Laties, Dept. of Radiation Biology & Biophysics,
  University of Rochester School of Medicine & Dentistry,
  Rochester, NY 14642
Publisher & Copyright: Society for the Experimental Analysis
  of Behavior, Inc.
Subscriptions: Instit. $22/yr. Indiv. $10/yr. Student $5/
  yr. Subscriptions available from Business Manager, Psy-
  chology Dept., Indiana University, Bloomington, IN 47401.
  Available on calendar year basis only. Bimonthly. Ca.
  4100. 190 pages/issue.

Description: "Primarily for the original publication of experiments relevant to the behavior of indiyidual organisms.
Review articles and theoretical papers will also be considered for publication."

Article Content: Operant conditioning: learning; motivation;
physiological psychology; experimental psychology; sensory psychology; animal behavior.

Typical Disciplines: Psychology; biology; physiology.

Intended Audience: Mainly advanced graduate students and
beginning graduate students, specialists and researchers,
also teachers.

Special Features: Research reports; theoretical articles;
book reviews; abstract for each article; abstracts also
printed on 3 x 5 cards that are then bound into each issue and are detachable; annual and cumulative index.

Acceptance/Rejection Criteria: Articles of high quality; clear
and concise.

Acceptance/Rejection Procedures: All articles are reviewed
by at least two referees, one or both of whom would be
a member of the Board of Editors; decisions to accept
or reject are made by the Editor or by one of the Associate Editors who serve as "action" editors of specific
MSS.

Manuscript Disposition: Receipt of MS acknowledged; about
two months required for a decision; rejected MS returned;
critique to author; 50% submitted MSS accepted; 100 MSS
published/yr.; 4 to 6 months from receipt of final version to publication; first accepted, first published.

Style Requirements: Consult January issue of journal; no preferred page length; 2 copies of MS; abstract of no more
than 200 words; do not use abbreviations; short, direct
statements; technical terms should be explained; favors
standard international system units (SI); cover page should
include title, authors, suggested running head (not more
than 50 characters and spaces), and key words (list in
order of importance, no more than 9, response under
study is next to last and experimental subject is last--
see Annual Subject Index); 2nd page contains author's
name, title, and affiliation and abstract; third and following pages contain introduction (not labelled) followed by
method, results, discussion; references, footnotes, tables
and figure legends go on separate pages.

Payment: None to or by author.

Reprints: 50 free; charge for additional depending on length
of article and number ordered.

Special Note: There will be a new editor in August, 1975.

73 JOURNAL OF EXPERIMENTAL EDUCATION (1932)

John Schmid, Dept. of Research and Statistical Methodology,
University of Northern Colorado, Greeley, CO 80631
Publisher & Copyright: Dembar Educational Research Ser-
vices, Inc., Box 1605, Madison, WI 53701
Subscriptions: Instit. & Indiv. $10/yr. Quarterly. Ca.
2000. 100 pages/issue.

Description: "Publishes specialized or technical educational
studies, treatises about the mathematics or methodology
of behavioral research, and monographs of major current
research interest."
Intended Audience: Students in psychology and education;
teachers; researchers; administrators; practitioners.
Special Features: Research reports; theoretical articles;
book reviews; hortatory or polemical articles; abstract
for each article; annual index; available on microform.

Acceptance/Rejection Criteria: Articles should generally
possess certain elements including a statement of the
problem; related research (minimal and selective); population and methodology; presentation of data; findings and
conclusion; summarizing statement.
Manuscript Disposition: 3 months required for decision; rejected MS returned; critique to author; 50% submitted
MSS accepted; 90-100 MSS published/yr.; 12-18 months
from acceptance to publication; first accepted, first published.
Style Requirements: Consult journal; preferred length 20
pages, double spaced; 2 copies of MS; abstract of not
more than 120 words; in a research paper abstract
should include statements of the problem, the method,
the data, and the conclusions; for review or discussion
article, abstract should state the topics covered and the
central thesis(es).
Payment: None to author; publisher charges a contributor's
fee of approximately $6 per printed page of about 1200
words, billed upon publication. Any major changes made
in the proofs that were not in original copy also charged
to author.
Reprints: 10 complimentary copies of journal issue; reprints
charged at cost.

74 JOURNAL OF EXPERIMENTAL PSYCHOLOGY

Publisher & Copyright: American Psychological Association,

1200 17th Street, N.W., Washington, D.C. 20036
This journal is undergoing extensive revision for 1975. It
will be published in four independently edited and distributed
sections. Members may subscribe singly or in self-selected
combinations. Some price advantage will go to those who
subscribe to more sections. Tentative page allocation to
JExP is 2400 pages, with 400 pages to the General section,
800 to Learning and Memory, 400 to Perception and Performance, and 400 to Animal Behavior Processes, with 400
in a "page bank" to be released to sections as needed. Please
consult the journal for further refinements and expansions.

The JOURNAL OF EXPERIMENTAL PSYCHOLOGY: GENERAL
Dr. Gregory A. Kimble, University of Colorado, Editor.†
Will publish articles in any area of experimental psychology when they are judged to present an integrative report
of new research leading to a substantial advance in knowledge. This includes, but is not limited to, articles such
as have appeared in JExP Monographs and as chapters in
contemporary books of "advances" in which authors present the theoretical-empirical implications of their own
research programs in a comprehensive fashion intelligible
to the general experimental psychologist.

The JOURNAL OF EXPERIMENTAL PSYCHOLOGY: LEARN-
ING AND MEMORY
Dr. Lyle E. Bourne, University of Colorado, Editor.†
Will publish experimental studies on fundamental learning
and memory processes in human behavior. This includes,
but is not limited to, the following topics: human conditioning; motor learning; complex discrimination learning;
sequential response and probability learning; verbal learning, transfer and retention; encoding strategies, insofar
as they are related to memory; learning to learn; concept formation and abstraction processes; problem solving;
deductive reasoning.

The JOURNAL OF EXPERIMENTAL PSYCHOLOGY: PERCEP-
TION AND PERFORMANCE
Dr. Michael I. Posner, University of Oregon, Editor.†
Will publish studies designed to foster understanding of
information processing operations and their relation to
experience and performance. This includes, but is not
limited to, the following topics: sensory transduction,
pattern recognition, perception, attention, motivation,
thinking, decision making, stress, and motor control.
Dependent variables may be response speed or accuracy,

thresholds, verbal protocols, autonomic or CNS activity, or other measures. Studies of perception and perform- ance are often closely linked to physiology and to engineer- ing applications, and contributions with these emphases are also encouraged.

The JOURNAL OF EXPERIMENTAL PSYCHOLOGY: ANIMAL BEHAVIOR PROCESSES
Dr. Allan R. Wagner, Yale University, Editor. †
Will publish experimental studies of basic mechanisms of perception, learning, motivation, and performance with infrahuman animals, in which the principal focus is on concepts and issues in general behavior theory. Animal experimental studies is thus reinstated as a major com- ponent of JExP.

†The four editors of the sections will also serve as members of the Board of Editors of JExP and will collaborate in es- tablishing standards of acceptance, allocation of articles to sections, and page allocations. It is expected that the sec- tions of JExP will maintain a publication lag of not greater than 12 months.

75 JOURNAL OF EXPERIMENTAL SOCIAL PSYCHOLOGY (1964)

Robert M. Krauss, Dept. of Psychology, Columbia University, Schermerhorn Hall, New York, N.Y. 10027
Publisher & Copyright: Academic Press, Inc., 111 5th Ave., New York, NY 10003
Subscriptions: Consult publishers. Monthly. Ca. 2000. 100 pages/issue.

Description: "Dedicated to the scientific investigation of so- cial interaction and related phenomenon. Reflects cur- rent significant research in various areas of social psy- chology. "
Article Content: Attitude change; group decision making; so- cial perception; attribution processes; social interaction.
Typical Disciplines: Social psychologists; psychologists; soci- ologists; administrative scientists.
Intended Audience: Beginning and advanced graduate students (in psychology); researchers.
Special Features: Research reports; theoretical articles; lit- erature reviews; abstract for each article; annual index; advertising.

Acceptance/Rejection Criteria: Main criteria are theoretical contributions and methodological soundness. Other criteria are novelty of findings or procedures and quality of writing.

Acceptance/Rejection Procedures: MSS are evaluated by one or more external reviewers. Final decision by editor.

Manuscript Disposition: Receipt of MS acknowledged; 2 months or more required for decision; rejected MS returned; critique to author; 10-20% submitted MSS accepted; 60 MSS published/yr.; 4-5 months from acceptance to publication; first accepted, first published.

Style Requirements: APA Publication Manual and consult journal; no page length limitations; 2 copies of MS; abstract of 100-200 words required.

Payment: None to or by author for publication.

Reprints: 50 free. Additional available at charge.

76 JGE: THE JOURNAL OF GENERAL EDUCATION (1946)

Robert and Caroline Eckhardt, 215 Wagner Building, Penn State University, University Park, PA 16802

Publisher & Copyright: The Pennsylvania State University Press

Subscriptions: Instit. & Indiv. $9/yr. Special rates for 3-year subscriptions. Quarterly. Ca. 1900. 104 pages/issue.

Description: "Articles that will be helpful to teachers, particularly of undergraduates and post-high-school pupils, and to administrators of colleges, junior colleges, and universities are published in JGE. Specialists who want to explain their findings to non-specialists find JGE a good place to publish."

Intended Audience: Broad range from general public to undergraduate and graduate students and teachers, researchers, and administrators. All disciplines represented.

Special Features: Theoretical articles; book reviews; letters to the editor; editorials; literature reviews; annual and cumulative index; available on microform; advertising.

Acceptance/Rejection Procedures: Readers from editorial board make recommendations to editors. The various issues of JGE are planned as units. MSS which do not fit into plans for next several numbers are returned.

Manuscript Disposition: Receipt of MS acknowledged; 4 weeks required for decision; "blind" refereeing; rejected MS

returned; 25% submitted MSS accepted; 28 MSS published/
yr.; 1 year from acceptance to publication.
Style Requirements: Chicago Manual of Style; no length requirements (because of nature of JGE, articles that are
longer or shorter than usual periodical length can be
published); 1 copy of MS; abstract not required.
Payment: None to or by author.
Reprints: 25 available without charge; no additional copies
available.

77 JOURNAL OF GENERAL PSYCHOLOGY (1927)

Warren H. Teichner (New Mexico State University)
Editorial Address: Managing Editor, The Journal Press, 2
Commercial Street, Provincetown, MA 02657
Publisher & Copyright: The Journal Press
Subscriptions: Instit. & Indiv. $26/yr. Special teachers'
and students' edition subscriptions available. Subscrip-
tions accepted on either a calendar year (Jan.-Dec.) or
July-June basis. Quarterly. Ca. 1700. 170 pages/is-
sue.

Description: "Devoted to experimental, physiological, and
comparative psychology. Human and animal laboratory
studies, and mathematical and other theoretical investigations are appropriate. Technological reports of significance to these areas are welcome."
Intended Audience: Mainly Ph.D. psychologists.
Special Features: Research reports; theoretical articles; letters to the editor; literature reviews; briefly reported
replications, refinements, and comments; abstract for
each article.

Acceptance/Rejection Criteria: Only criteria that the articles
be professionally done and make some contribution to the
literature.
Acceptance/Rejection Procedures: Final decision rests with
the Managing Editor on the basis of two reports: one
from the Editor or a member of the Editorial Board on
the merits and significance of the MS, and one from the
Copy Editing Department on the mechanical, editorial,
and stylistic problems involved in publishing the paper.
Manuscript Disposition: Receipt of MS acknowledged; 1 month
required for decision; rejected MS returned; critique to
author (usually); 40% submitted MSS accepted; 60 MSS
published/yr.; 9-12 months from acceptance to publication;
first accepted, first published.

Style Requirements: Consult journal; preferred length 10-20
pages, double spaced or 2500-5000 words; minimum length
2 pages or 500 words; no maximum length; original plus
one copy of MS; abstract required at beginning of text for
all articles over 500 words; proper sequence is text,
references, footnotes, tables, figures, and figure legends;
all copy double spaced; enclose a submission letter with
a statement that the MS is not under consideration elsewhere and giving credentials.

Payment: None to author; author is not charged for straight
text material; nominal charge is made for tables, figures,
complicated equations, or excessive use of special fonts.

Reprints: 100 free; price list sent with page proof for additional reprints.

78 JOURNAL OF GENETIC PSYCHOLOGY (1891)
formerly The Pedagogical Seminary

John E. Horrocks (Ohio State University)
Editorial Address: Managing Editor, The Journal Press, 2
Commercial Street, Provincetown, MA 02657
Publisher & Copyright: The Journal Press
Subscriptions: Instit. & Indiv. $26/yr. Special teacher &
student edition subscriptions available. Subscriptions
accepted on either a calendar-year or a July-June basis.
Quarterly, starting March. Ca. 1650. 190 pages/issue.

Description: "Devoted to developmental and clinical psychology."
Intended Audience: Mainly Ph.D. psychologists.
Special Features: Research reports; theoretical articles; book
reviews; letters to the editor; literature reviews; briefly
reported replications and refinements; abstract for each
issue.

Acceptance/Rejection Criteria: Only criteria that the articles
be professionally done and make some contribution to the
literature.
Acceptance/Rejection Procedures: Final decision rests with
the Managing Editor on the basis of two reports: one
from the Editor or a member of the Editorial Board on
the merits and significance of the MS, and one from the
Copy Editing Department on the mechanical, editorial,
and stylistic problems involved in publishing the paper.
Manuscript Disposition: Receipt of MS acknowledged; 1 month
required for decision; rejected MS returned; critique to

author (usually); 40% of submitted MSS accepted; 65 MSS
published/yr.; 12 to 15 months from acceptance to publication; first accepted, first published.

Style Requirements: Consult journal; preferred length 10-20
pages or 2500-5000 words; minimum length 2 pages or
500 words; no maximum length; all copy double spaced;
original plus one copy of MS; abstract required at beginning of text for all articles over 500 words; enclose
a submission letter with a statement that the MS is not
under consideration elsewhere and giving credentials; do
not begin a sentence with a numeral; do not fold MS.

Payment: None to author; author is not charged for straight
text material. Nominal charge is made for tables,
figures, complicated equations, or excessive use of special fonts.

Reprints: 100 free. Price list sent with page proof for additional reprints.

79 JOURNAL OF HIGHER EDUCATION (1930)

Robert J. Silverman, (Ohio State University) 2070 Neil Ave.,
Columbus, OH 43210

Publisher: The Ohio State University Press, same address
as above.

Organizational Affiliation of Journal: American Association
for Higher Education (AAHE).

Subscriptions: Instit. $12/yr. Indiv. non-member $10/yr.
Indiv. member AAHE $8/yr. Students $8/yr. Issued
9 times/yr., excluding summer. Ca. 5800. 88 pages/
issue.

Description: "To bring to the attention of the higher educational community, broadly conceived, articles which by
focusing on processes, structure, and dynamics of higher
education will improve operations and broaden understanding."

Article Content: Administrative behavior; evaluation; finance;
legal issues; philosophy of higher education; learning;
MSS favored which deal with the implications of research
studies on higher education, discuss emerging policy problems and issues, examine existing concepts and analyze
concepts that seem to be outmoded, and report on case
studies which have significant implications subject to gen-
eralization.

Intended Audience: Students; teachers; researchers; administrators; practitioners; those who have a special interest
in higher education.

Special Features: See article content; book reviews; editorials; special themes twice a year; annual ·index.

Acceptance/Rejection Criteria: Originality; applicability to problems in field; significance to readers; contribution to higher education as a field of study; contribution to basic knowledge; clarity and precision of writing; logical development of argument; appropriateness of treatment to author's stated objectives; appropriate use of theory/statistics; accuracy; thoroughness; substantiation where necessary; style and language familiar to everyone; article should be able to stand by itself; not submitted elsewhere.

Acceptance/Rejection Procedures: MSS reviewed in editorial office and those falling low in the criteria are rejected and notification to authors occurs within 2 weeks. Those papers "with promise" are sent to reviewers for recommendation.

Manuscript Disposition: Receipt of MS acknowledged; 4-6 weeks required for decision; "blind" refereeing; rejected MS returned; critique to author (for 30% of MSS); 8% submitted MSS accepted; 50-55 MSS published/yr.; 3-6 months from acceptance to publication; first accepted, first published.

Style Requirements: Manual of the University of Chicago Press and journal; preferred length no less than five nor more than 20 typed pages, double spaced; 3 copies of MS, including original; broad margins on left; no abstract; include stamped, self-addressed envelope.

Payments: None to author; author pays for corrections that exceed 10% of cost of article.

Reprints: Available at charge from printer.

80 JOURNAL OF THE HISTORY OF THE BEHAVIORAL SCIENCES (1965)

Robert I. Watson, Psychology Dept., Conant Hall, University of New Hampshire, Durham, NH 03824 (new editor in 1975).

Publisher & Copyright: Clinical Psychology Publishing Co., 4 Conant Square, Brandon, VT 05733

Subscriptions: Instit. $20/yr. Indiv. $15/yr. Quarterly. Ca. 1000. 400 pages/issue.

Description: "Interdisciplinary journal of the history of the behavioral sciences."

<u>Typical Disciplines:</u> Psychologists; psychiatrists; physiologists; sociologists; anthropologists; philosophers; educators.

<u>Intended Audience:</u> Teachers; researchers; administrators; practitioners; people in above disciplines.

<u>Special Features:</u> Research reports; theoretical articles; book reviews; letters to the editor; editorials; semi-annual bibliographies; annual index.

<u>Acceptance/Rejection Criteria:</u> Historical (i. e., not summaries of recent past--10-20 years); behavioral emphasis; originality; use of primary sources; organized; not digressive; non-doctrinaire; "fair."

<u>Acceptance/Rejection Procedures:</u> Sent to either a member of the editorial board or a specially selected knowledgeable referee. In case of doubt two or more opinions, other than editor's, obtained; editor has final decision.

<u>Manuscript Disposition:</u> Receipt of MS acknowledged; 6 months required for decision; rejected MS returned; critique to author; accepted MS not returned with galley; 50% submitted MSS accepted; 24 MSS published/yr.; 12 months from acceptance to publication; first accepted, first published.

<u>Style Requirements:</u> Consult journal; preferred length 10 pages, double spaced; maximum length 25 pages; 2 copies of MS; no abstract; lengthy quote should be indented in text and double-spaced; use numbers in parentheses to identify references rather than date of publication; references should be alphabetized and grouped at the end of the MS; footnotes should be identified by number superscripts and grouped at the end of the MS, although they will be inserted on the appropriate printed page.

<u>Payment:</u> None to author; page charges will be initiated in 1975.

<u>Reprints:</u> Available at charge.

81   JOURNAL OF HUMANISTIC PSYCHOLOGY (1961)

Thomas C. Greening, 1314 Westwood Blvd., Los Angeles, CA 90024

<u>Publisher & Copyright:</u> Association for Humanistic Psychology

<u>Subscriptions:</u> Instit. $10/yr. Indiv. non-member $8/yr. No charge for members. Available on calendar year basis only. Quarterly. Ca. 5000. 80 pages/issue.

<u>Description:</u> "Is the journal of the Association for Humanistic Psychology. It is concerned with the publication of

experiential reports, theoretical papers, research studies, applications of humanistic psychology, and humanistic analyses of contemporary culture."

Article Content: Topics of special interest are authenticity, encounter, self-actualization, search for meaning, creativity, intentionality, psychological health, being motivation, values, love, identity, and commitment.

Intended Audience: General public; students; teachers; researchers; administrators; practitioners

Special Features: See description; literature reviews; description of authors.

Acceptance/Rejection Criteria: Clarity; relevance to humanistic psychology; originality.

Acceptance/Rejection Procedures: Editor reads; if he is undecided, he sends MS to one or more reviewers.

Manuscript Disposition: Receipt of MS acknowledged; 2 months required for decision; rejected MS returned; critique to author; 10% submitted MSS accepted; 35 MSS published/yr.; 3 months from acceptance to publication.

Style Requirements: APA Publication Manual and journal; preferred length from 2 to 30 pages, double spaced; 2 copies of MS; no abstract.

Payment: None to or by authors.

Reprints: 100 free.

82 JOURNAL OF INDIVIDUAL PSYCHOLOGY (1940)
    formerly Individual Psychology Bulletin, Vols. 1-9; American Journal of Individual Psychology, Vols. 10-12

Dr. Raymond J. Corsini, 140 Niuiki Circle, Honolulu, Hawaii 96821

Publisher & Copyright: American Society of Adlerian Psychology, Inc.

Subscriptions: $5/yr. Semi-annually in May and Nov. Ca. 1400. 125 pages/issue. Business Office address is Journal of Individual Psychology, Dept. of Psychology, John Dewey Hall, University of Vermont, Burlington, VT 05401

Description: "Devoted to a holistic, phenomenological, teleological, field-theoretical, and socially oriented approach to psychology and related fields. This approach is based on the assumption of the uniqueness, self-consistency, activity, and creativity of the human individual; an open dynamic system of motivation; and an innate potentiality for social living. Endeavors to continue the tradition of Alfred Adler's Individual Psychology."

Article Content: Personality theory; psychotherapy; clinical psychology; counseling.

Intended Audience: Clinical psychologists; counselors; graduate students; psychiatrists; social workers; teachers; researchers; paraprofessionals.

Special Features: Research reports; theoretical articles; book reviews; letters to the editor; editorials; hortatory or polemical articles; literature reviews; program of annual meeting of American Society of Adlerian Psychology, Inc., various reports, and news notes of the organization and its affiliated society; annual and cumulative index; advertising.

Acceptance/Rejection Criteria: In general, only original papers are published.

Manuscript Disposition: Receipt of MS acknowledged; 4 months required for decision; rejected MS returned; critique to author; 30% submitted MSS accepted; 25 to 30 MSS published/yr.; 2 months from acceptance to publication; first accepted, first published.

Style Requirements: APA Publication Manual; no set page length requirements; all copy double-spaced; two copies of MS; abstract desirable; subheadings requested.

Payment: None to or by author.

Reprints: Must be requested on provided order blank; furnished two weeks after publication of MS.

83 JOURNAL OF MATHEMATICAL PSYCHOLOGY (1962)

J. E. Keith Smith, Department of Psychology, University of Michigan, Ann Arbor, MI 48104

Publisher & Copyright: Academic Press Inc., 111 5th Ave., New York, NY 10003

Subscriptions: Instit. & Indiv. $35/yr. Quarterly. Ca. 1200. 150 pages/issue.

Description: "To publish research in mathematical psychology; either mathematical work on models relevant to behavioral observations or empirical work to investigate the validity of mathematical models."

Article Content: Psychophysics; mathematical learning; concept formation; psycholinguistics; economic choice behavior.

Typical Disciplines: Psychology; statistics; mathematics;

economics; artificial intelligence.

Intended Audience: Advanced graduate students and specialists; teachers; researchers.

Special Features: Research reports; theoretical articles; abstract for each article.

Acceptance/Rejection Criteria: Relevance; rigor; clarity; originality.

Acceptance/Rejection Procedures: All MSS assigned to Board of Editors. Editor chooses 0, 1, or 2 referees and makes decision.

Manuscript Disposition: Receipt of MS acknowledged; 5 months from receipt to decision; rejected MS returned; critique to author; 50% of submitted MSS accepted; 20 MSS published/yr.; 4 months from acceptance to publication; first accepted, first published.

Style Requirements: Consult journal; no page length requirements; 2 copies of MS; abstract required.

Payment: None to or by author.

Reprints: 50 free.

84 JOURNAL OF MOTOR BEHAVIOR (1969)

Richard Schmidt, Barbour Gymnasium, University of Michigan, Ann Arbor, MI 48104

Publisher: Rood Associates, 726 State St., Santa Barbara, CA 93101

Subscriptions: Instit. $25/yr. Indiv. $10/yr. Quarterly. Ca. 1000. 80 pages/issue.

Description: "The journal published papers which contribute to a basic understanding of human motor behavior, broadly defined."

Article Content: Papers concerned with motor learning and skilled performance predominate, but studies of other factors such as kinesthetic perception, fatigue, growth and maturation, and anthropometric variables as they relate to human motor behavior are acceptable.

Typical Disciplines: Psychology; physical education; industrial engineering.

Intended Audience: Students; researchers; people in above mentioned disciplines.

Special Features: Research reports; theoretical articles; literature reviews; notes and comments section devoted to replications, criticisms, replies, or shorter papers presenting new and stimulating ideas; abstract for each article.

Acceptance/Rejection Criteria: Animal and applied work are acceptable to the extent that they contribute to a basic understanding of human motor behavior; work on motor performance which is clearly directed toward the solution of physiological problems is beyond the scope of the journal.

Acceptance/Rejection Procedures: Critical review by one Associate Editor. A member of the Editorial Board then summarizes and modifies the review and recommendations are sent to the Managing Editor.

Manuscript Disposition: Receipt of MS acknowledged; 8 weeks required for decision; rejected MS returned; critique to author; 50% submitted MSS accepted; 32 MSS published/yr.; 4 months from acceptance to publication; first accepted, first published.

Style Requirements: APA Publication Manual; preferred length 5-20 pages; no minimum or maximum length; double space all copy; 3 copies of MS; abstract of 50 to 150 words.

Payment: None to or by author.

Reprints: Ordered at cost of printing ($16/4 pages, 100 reprints).

85 JOURNAL OF PERSONALITY

Philip R. Costanzo, Psychology Department, Duke University, Durham, North Carolina 27706

Publisher & Copyright: Duke University Press, Box 6697, College Station, Durham, North Carolina

Subscriptions: $12/yr. Quarterly. Yearly Vol. 700 pages.

Description: "Devoted to scientific investigations in the field of personality. Scope not fixed, and is intended to reflect areas of current significant research."

Article Content: Current stress on experimental studies of behavior dynamics and character structure, personality-related consistencies in cognitive processes and development of personality in its cultural context.

Acceptance/Rejection Criteria: Most contributions empirical.

Style Requirements: APA Publication Manual; maximum length 20 pages, double spaced; 2 copies of MS.

Payment: None to author; authors pay excess page charge of $15 for each journal page over 20.

Reprints: 50 offprints free; additional reprints available at cost.

86 JOURNAL OF PERSONALITY ASSESSMENT
formerly, Journal of Projective Techniques & Personality
Assessment

Walter G. Klopfer, Portland State University, 7840 S.W. 51st
Ave., Portland, OR 97219
Publisher & Copyright: Society for Personality Assessment
Subscriptions: Instit. & Indiv. $15/yr. Order from Mrs.
Marilyn Wier, 1070 E. Angeleno Ave., Burbank, CA
91501. Six issues per year. 100 pages/issue.

Description: "Is the official organ of the Society for Personality Assessment, a non-profit corporation for the study
and advancement of projective and other assessment
techniques."
Typical Disciplines: Psychologists; psychiatrists.
Intended Audience: Teachers; researchers; administrators;
practitioners; students.
Special Features: Research reports; theoretical articles;
book reviews; literature reviews; abstract for each article;
annual index; advertising.

Acceptance/Rejection Criteria: Significant contribution to the
area; clarity and conciseness; required style.
Acceptance/Rejection Procedures: All MSS are forwarded to
two consulting editors; upon receipt of the evaluated MS,
Editor weighs evaluations and makes an editorial decision.
Manuscript Disposition: Receipt of MS acknowledged; 1 to
1 1/2 months from receipt of MS to decision; "blind"
refereeing; rejected MS returned; critique to author; 40%
submitted MSS accepted; 65 MSS published/yr.; 16 months
from acceptance to publication; first accepted, first published.
Style Requirements: APA Publication Manual and journal; no
preferred length; 2 copies of MS; abstract of 100-120
words required.
Payment: None to author; authors pay for tabular material
(illustrations, tables, figures, special type) at the printer's cost of $.75 per column inch.
Reprints: Ordered with galley proofs at price determined by
length of MS.

87 JOURNAL OF PERSONALITY AND SOCIAL PSYCHOLOGY

John T. Lanzetta, Department of Psychology, Dartmouth College, Hanover, NH 03755

Publisher & Copyright: American Psychological Association, 1200 17th Street, N. W. , Washington, D. C. 20036
Subscriptions: $48/yr. Available on a Jan.-Dec. basis only. Monthly, 4 vols./yr., 3 issues/vol. 142 pages/ issue. Ca. 4700.

Description: "Publishes original research reports in the areas of social psychology and personality dynamics. "
Article Content: Basic research & theory in the broad areas of social interaction & group processes. Specifically, interpersonal perception and attitude change; psychological aspects of formal social systems and less structured collective phenomena; socialization process at both the child and adult levels; social motivation and personality; relation of personality to group process and social systems.
Intended Audience: Teachers; researchers; students; people in social psychology.
Special Features: Research reports; abstract for each article; issue and volume index; advertising.

Acceptance/Rejection Criteria: Priority given to reports which make substantial and significant contributions to the literature. Methodological articles, studies primarily concerned with the development of measuring instruments, replications, and reports of negative results or failures to replicate published work are acceptable if judged to make a substantial contribution to knowledge. MSS in these categories should be brief (not more than nine type-written pages) so they can be published as short reports.
Acceptance/Rejection Procedures: Three associate editors take full responsibility for a portion of the MSS.
Manuscript Disposition: Receipt of MS acknowledged; 11 weeks from receipt to decision; "blind" refereeing; rejected MS returned; critique to author; 24% submitted MSS accepted; 210 articles published/yr.; 13 months from acceptance to publication; first accepted, first published.
Style Requirements: APA Publication Manual and journal; maximum length 45 pages, double spaced; 2 copies of MS; abstract of 120 words or less, typed on a separate page; title should be 15 words or less.
Payment: None to or by author.
Reprints: Ordered at charge from the printer when galleys received.

88 JOURNAL OF PHENOMENOLOGICAL PSYCHOLOGY (1970)
    Studies in the Sciences of Human Experience and Behavior

Amedeo Giorgi (English Lang. Editor) Psychology Department,
    Duquesne University, Pittsburgh, PA 15219
Publisher & Copyright: Duquesne University Press, Univer-
    sity Hall, Pittsburgh, PA 15219
Subscriptions: Instit. & Indiv. $9/yr. Issued twice a year.
    140 pages/issue.

Description: "... dedicated to the aim of approaching psy-
    chology in such a way that the entire range of experience
    and behavior of man as a human person may be properly
    studied in a rigorous way."
Typical Disciplines: Psychology; philosophy; sociology.
Intended Audience: Teachers; researchers; practitioners;
    students.
Special Features: Theoretical articles; book reviews; cumu-
    lative index; advertising.

Acceptance/Rejection Criteria: Scholarly analysis of a psy-
    chological problem from a phenomenological perspective
    (broadly interpreted); articles may be theoretical or em-
    pirical, academic or applied, clinical or experimental,
    individual or social, just so they reflect an attempt to
    approach man as he actually experiences and behaves in
    the world; fidelity to the phenomenon of man as a whole.
Acceptance/Rejection Procedures: All MSS are read by at
    least 3 readers and consensus determines publication.
Manuscript Disposition: Receipt of MS acknowledged; 6 months
    required for decision; rejected MS returned (one copy);
    60% submitted MSS accepted; 12 MSS published/yr.; 1
    year from acceptance to publication.
Style Requirements: Consult journal; no preferred length; 3
    copies of MS; abstract not required.
Payment: None to or by author.
Reprints: 25 free.

89 JOURNAL OF PSYCHOLOGY (1935) The General Field of
    Psychology

Managing Editor, The Journal Press, 2 Commercial Street,
    Provincetown, MA 02657
Publisher & Copyright: The Journal Press
Subscriptions: Instit. & Indiv. $39/yr. Special Teachers &
    Students edition subscriptions available. Subscriptions

accepted on either a calendar-year basis or a July-through-June basis. Bimonthly, starting January. Ca. 1750. 190 pages/issue.

Description: "Specializes in very rapid publication and, in general, covers the same fields as Journal of Social Psychology, Journal of General Psychology, and Journal of Genetic Psychology."
Intended Audience: Typical readers and contributors are Ph.D. psychologists.
Special Features: Research reports; theoretical articles; literature reviews; abstract for each article.

Acceptance/Rejection Criteria: Only criteria are that the articles be professionally done and make some contribution to the literature.
Acceptance/Rejection Procedures: Final decision rests with the managing editor on the basis of two reports: one from the editor or a member of the editorial board on the merits and significance of the MS, and one from the Copy Editing Department on the mechanical, editorial, and stylistic problems involved in publishing the paper. Acceptance procedures are made as rapidly as possible.
Manuscript Disposition: Receipt of MS acknowledged; 1 to 2 weeks required for decision; rejected MS returned; critique to author (usually); 40% submitted MSS accepted; 120 MSS published/yr.; 1-2 months from acceptance to publication; first accepted, first published.
Style Requirements: Consult journal; no definite page length limits; original typewritten version of MS plus one copy; summary required at beginning of text for all articles over 500 words; double space all lines; do not fold MS; do not begin a sentence with a numeral; proper sequence is text, references, footnotes, tables, figures, and figure legends; enclose a submission letter giving credentials and stating that MS is not under consideration elsewhere.
Payment: None to author; immediate publication page charges paid by authors are based on $60 per 4-page signature. Nominal charges are also made for tables, figures, complicated equations, etc.
Reprints: 200 free; price list sent with page proof.

90 JOURNAL OF RESEARCH AND DEVELOPMENT IN EDUCATION

Editor, G-3 Aderhold Building, College of Education, Univer-

sity of Georgia, Athens, Georgia 30602
Publisher & Copyright: College of Education, University of
Georgia, Athens, Georgia 30602
Subscriptions: $7/yr. Available from Editor, G-3 Aderhold
Building, College of Education, University of Georgia,
Athens, Georgia 30602. Annual subscriptions automatical-
ly renewed unless subscriber cancels. Issued 5/yr. in
Fall, Winter, Spring, Summer and monograph supplement.

Description: "Each issue is devoted to a central theme in
education and covers research and development in that
area."
Article Content: Higher education--an emerging discipline
and need for reform; innovating academic bureaucracy;
organization for research--new patterns, new perspectives;
leadership roles in educational innovation; accountability.

Acceptance/Rejection Criteria: Editorial board selects theme
for each issue. Criteria for theme selection are rele-
vancy, breadth of interest and availability of scholarly
collaboration on a broad geographical basis. Theme suggestions from scholars, researchers, and developers as
well as professional organizations in education welcome.
Unsolicited MSS must be accompanied by postage-paid
return envelope.

91 JOURNAL OF RESEARCH IN PERSONALITY (1965)
formerly Journal of Experimental Research in Personality

Jerry S. Wiggins, Department of Psychology, University of
British Columbia, Vancouver 8, B.C. Canada
Publisher & Copyright: Academic Press, Inc., 111 5th Ave.,
New York 10003
Subscriptions: Instit. $22/yr. Indiv. $10/yr. Quarterly.
Ca. 1000. 80 pages/issue. Subscriptions available on
calendar-year basis only.

Description: "To publish studies in the field of personality
and in related fields basic to the understanding of personality. Subject matter includes treatments of genetic,
physiological, motivational, learning, perceptual, cognitive, and social processes of both normal and abnormal
kinds in both human and animal subjects."
Intended Audience: Teachers; researchers; practitioners; students.
Typical Disciplines: Psychology.

Special Features: Research reports; theoretical articles; hortatory or polemical articles; abstract for each article; annual index; brief notes and critiques.

Acceptance/Rejection Criteria: Equal emphasis is placed on experimental and descriptive research, with preference given to presentations of an integrated series of independent studies concerned with significant theoretical issues relating to personality. Also publishes theoretical articles and critical reviews of current experimental and methodological interest.

Acceptance/Rejection Procedures: Each MS is processed by the Editor or one of two Associate Editors. The MS is reviewed independently by at least one Consulting Editor who may be a member of the Editorial Board of who may be an outside reviewer used on an ad hoc basis. Thus each MS is reviewed by at least two and frequently three independent reviewers.

Manuscript Disposition: Receipt of MS acknowledged; 3 months required for decision; rejected MS returned; critique to author; 25% submitted MSS accepted; 60 MSS published/yr.; 4-6 months from acceptance to publication; first accepted, first published.

Style Requirements: Consult journal; no set minimum or maximum length; length determined by nature of material reported; "dissertation" and other excessive writing styles unacceptable; 2 copies of MS; abstract required.

Payment: None to or by author.

Reprints: 50 free.

92 JOURNAL OF SOCIAL PSYCHOLOGY (1929)

Leonard W. Doob (Yale University). Editorial Address: Managing Editor, The Journal Press, 2 Commercial Street, Provincetown, MA 02657

Publisher & Copyright: The Journal Press

Subscriptions: Instit. & Indiv. $39/yr. Special teacher & student editions subscriptions available. Subscriptions accepted on either a calendar-year or a July-June basis. Bimonthly, starting Feb. Ca. 2400. 190 pages/issue.

Description: "Devoted to studies of persons in group settings and of culture and personality. Special consideration is given to studies reporting research which tests hypotheses in other cultures or which is based upon field work of an experimental or empirical character."

Intended Audience: Mainly PhD psychologists.
Special Features: Research reports; theoretical articles; letters to the editor; literature reviews; briefly reported replications and refinements; abstract for each issue.

Acceptance/Rejection Criteria: Only criteria that the articles be professionally done and make some contribution to the literature. However, the following safeguards are recommended: specify the national, cultural, and educational provenance or background of the subjects or informants; generalizations and conclusions should contain qualifying phrases or clauses which clearly suggest that only a portion of mankind has been sampled; analyses of results should be placed in the present tense only when there is no doubt that reference is being made to the subjects or informants of the investigation; otherwise the past tense is mandatory.
Acceptance/Rejection Procedures: Final decision rests with the Managing Editor on the basis of two reports: one from the Editor or a member of the Editorial Board on the merits and significance of the MS, and one from the Copy Editing Department on the mechanical, editorial, and stylistic problems involved in publishing the paper.
Manuscript Disposition: Receipt of MS acknowledged; 2-4 weeks required for decision; rejected MS returned; critique to author (usually); 40% submitted MSS accepted; 100 MSS published/yr.; 1 year from acceptance to publication; first accepted, first published.
Style Requirements: Consult journal; preferred length 10-20 pages or 2500-5000 words; minimum length 2 pages or 500 words; no maximum length; all copy double spaced; original plus one copy of MS; abstract required at beginning of text for all articles over 500 words; enclose a submission letter with a statement that the MS is not under consideration elsewhere and giving credentials.
Payment: None to author; author is not charged for straight text material; nominal charge is made for tables, figures, complicated equations, or excessive use of special fonts.
Reprints: 100 free. Price list sent with page proof for additional reprints.

93 JOURNAL OF TRANSPERSONAL PSYCHOLOGY (1969)

Anthony Sutich, Box 4437, Stanford, CA 94305
Publisher & Copyright: Transpersonal Institute
Subscriptions: $7.50/yr. Issued twice a year. Ca. 2500.

100 pages/issue. Order subscriptions from editorial address.

<u>Description:</u> "Journal is concerned with the publication of theoretical and applied research, original contributions, empirical papers, articles and studies in meta-needs, ultimate values, unitive consciousness, peak experiences, ecstasy, mystical experience, B values, essence, bliss, awe, wonder, self-actualization of everyday life, oneness, cosmic awareness, cosmic play, individual and species-wide synergy, the theories and practices of meditation, transcendental phenomena, spiritual paths, responsiveness, compassion, and related concepts, experiences and activities."

<u>Typical Disciplines:</u> Therapists; teachers; philosophers; religious and spiritual teachers.

<u>Intended Audience:</u> General public.

<u>Special Features:</u> Research reports; theoretical articles; book reviews.

<u>Acceptance/Rejection Criteria:</u> Excellent, useful articles; no other explicit criteria.

<u>Acceptance/Rejection Procedures:</u> Editor reads MS, passes it on to several other editors; if response generally favorable, several editors discuss it.

<u>Manuscript Disposition:</u> Receipt of MS acknowledged; 3 months required for decision; rejected MS returned; critique to author; 20% submitted MSS accepted; 12 MSS published/yr.; 4 months from acceptance to publication; first accepted, first published.

<u>Style Requirements:</u> No specific statement, but see back issues of journal; no preferred length; 2 copies of MS; abstract not specifically required, but appreciated; readable, not scholastic, style.

<u>Payment:</u> None to or by author.

<u>Reprints:</u> 50 free; additional charge depending on length and number of reprints.

94 JOURNAL OF VERBAL LEARNING AND VERBAL BEHAVIOR (1962)

Edwin Martin, Human Performance Center, University of Michigan, 330 Packard, Ann Arbor, MI

<u>Publisher & Copyright:</u> Academic Press, 111 5th Ave. NY 10003

<u>Subscriptions:</u> Instit. $32/yr. Write publisher for individual

rates.   Bimonthly.   Ca. 2300.   125 pages/issue.

Description: "Publishes original theoretical, review, and experimental papers in the area of human memory and verbal learning, psycholinguistics, and other closely related
   verbal processes."
Intended Audience: Teachers; researchers; advanced students
   in the areas of human memory, psycholinguistics, verbal
   learning.
Special Features: Research reports; theoretical articles; abstract for each article; annual index.

Acceptance/Rejection Criteria: Significance of problem and
   preciseness of its statement; linkage of problem with
   previous relevant work; credibility of relation between
   stated problem and experimental design; adequacy of ex-
   periment per se; appropriateness and sufficiency of data
   analyses; clarity of relation between problem-design-re-
   sults package as whole; compliance with style requirements (or MS may be returned without evaluation); published papers are expected to make a significant contribution to shaping of scientific issues and theories; a paper
   that is primarily a record of completed experimental
   work is not appropriate.
Acceptance/Rejection Procedures: MSS evaluated by either
   Editor or Associate Editor plus selected members of
   Editorial Board.
Manuscript Disposition: Receipt of MS acknowledged; 30 days
   required for decision; "blind" refereeing on request; rejected MS returned; critique to author; 20% submitted
   MSS accepted; 75 MSS published/yr.; 7 months from acceptance to publication; first accepted, first published.
Style Requirements: APA Publication Manual and journal; no
   preferred length; 4 copies of MS; abstract not exceeding
   120 words; page 1 should contain article title, author's
   name, complete affiliation, and at bottom of page a short
   title not exceeding 45 characters and spaces and also the
   name and mailing address (including zip) of person receiving proofs; page 2 should contain title and author's
   name and for Annual Subject Index 2 or 3 items describing topic (each item should suggest a two-level entry con-
   sisting of general & specific topics--see Subject Index in
   December issue); page 3 contains abstract; page 4 begins
   text with no heading; avoid almost all abbreviations.
Payment: None to or by author.
Reprints: 50 free; additional available at charge.

95 JOURNAL OF VOCATIONAL BEHAVIOR (1971)

Samuel H. Osipow, Dept. of Psychology, 1945 N. High St.,
Columbus, OH 43210
Publisher & Copyright: Academic Press, Inc., 111 5th Ave.,
N. Y. 10003
Subscriptions: Instit. & Indiv. $25/yr. Quarterly. Ca.
1000. 125 pages/issue.

Description: "Publishes empirical, methodological, and theoretical articles related to such issues as the validation of
theoretical constructs, developments in instrumentation,
program comparisons, and research methodology as related to vocational development, preference, choice and
selection, implementation, satisfaction, and effectiveness
throughout the life span and across cultural, national,
sex, and other demographic boundaries."
Typical Disciplines: Psychology; education; sociology; pos-
sibly labor economics; business (personnel & management).
Intended Audience: Teachers; researchers; administrators;
practitioners; students.
Special Features: Research reports; theoretical articles; literature reviews; abstract for each article; annual index.

Acceptance/Rejection Criteria: Literature reviews and descriptions of program applications will be published on
occasion. Long reports describing an integrated series
of studies as well as papers describing a single, cir-
cumscribed study will be published. Brief notes of a
methodological, instrumentation or replication nature
will also be considered.
Manuscript Disposition: Receipt of MS acknowledged; 2
months required for decision; "blind" refereeing; rejected MS returned; critique to author; 50% submitted
MSS accepted; 50 MSS published/yr.; 10 months from
acceptance to publication; first accepted, first published.
Style Requirements: Consult journal; preferred length 10-20
pages double spaced; minimum length 2 pages, maximum
45 pages; 2 copies of MS; abstract required; first page
should contain the article title, author's name, affiliation
and address to which correspondence should be sent; authors should not place their name on the MS itself.
Payments: None to author; author charged for alterations in
excess of 10% of the cost of composition.
Reprints: 50 free.

96 LEARNING AND MOTIVATION (1970)

J. Bruce Overmier, Department of Psychology, 212 Elliott
    Hall, University of Minnesota, Minneapolis, MN 55455
Publisher & Copyright: Academic Press, Inc., 111 5th Ave.,
    NY 10003
Subscriptions: Instit. $29/yr. Indiv. $14/yr. Quarterly.
    125 pages/issue.

Description: "Publishes original experimental and theoretical
    papers addressed to the analysis of basic phenomena and
    mechanisms of learning and motivation, including papers
    on biological and evolutionary influences upon the learn-
    ing and motivation processes. Its goals are the promo-
    tion of basic research into the phenomena of learning and
    motivation and the development of integrative theory to
    account for the phenomena."
Article Content: Traditional papers on animal learning and
    motivation; ethological factors in the analysis of learning
    and motivation; biological constraints upon learning; re-
    search with human subjects which contributes to general
    psychological theory.
Intended Audience: Teachers; researchers; students; people
    in fields of psychology, ethology, animal behavior.
Special Features: Research reports; theoretical articles;
    brief notes describing important new methods and tech-
    niques for studying or quantifying phenomena of learning
    and motivation; abstract for each article; annual index.

Acceptance/Rejection Criteria: Must make a substantial con-
    tribution to understanding of basic principles of learning
    and motivation and to general behavior theory; preference
    given to longer, more substantive papers.
Acceptance/Rejection Procedures: Editor or Associate Edi-
    tor serves as "Action Editor." Usually two ad hoc re-
    views are obtained from specialists in topical area of
    MS.
Manuscript Disposition: Receipt of MS acknowledged; 3-4
    months required for decision; "blind" refereeing upon re-
    quest; rejected MS returned; critique to author; 25% sub-
    mitted MSS accepted; 40-50 MSS published/yr.; 3-6
    months from acceptance to publication; first accepted,
    first published basis.
Style Requirements: APA Publication Manual and journal; no
    page length requirements; 4 complete copies of MS; au-
    thors desiring "blind" reviewing must submit two copies
    of MS free from identifying information; abstract required.

Payment: None to or by author.
Reprints: 50 free; charge for additional based on article
     length.

97 MEASUREMENT AND EVALUATION IN GUIDANCE (1967)

William A. Mehrens, Michigan State University, 460 Erickson
     Hall, East Lansing, MI 48823
Publisher & Copyright: American Personnel & Guidance Asso-
     ciation, 1607 New Hampshire N. W., Washington, D. C.
     20009
Subscriptions: Instit. & Indiv. non-member, $8/yr. Included
     in dues for members. Quarterly. Ca. 3000. 64 pages/
     issue.

Description: "Deals with theoretical and other problems of
     the measurement specialist as well as the measurement
     problems of the administrator, counselor, or personnel
     worker--in schools and colleges, public and private
     agencies, business, industry, and government. "
Article Content: Testing in general; measurement of ability,
     achievement, personality, interest, attitudes, values; col-
     lege environment; educational & career counseling research;
     culture-fair tests.
Intended Audience: Researchers; administrators; practitioners;
     some teachers; students.
Special Features: Research reports; theoretical articles; book
     reviews; letters to the editor; editorials; literature re-
     views; abstract for each article; annual index; available
     on microform; research in brief (2 pages, no tables;
     author makes data available on request); advertising.

Acceptance/Rejection Criteria: All MSS must have clearly
     described implications for the practitioner in measure-
     ment and evaluation.
Acceptance/Rejection Procedures: Usually blind reviewing by
     two reviewers; comments, worked MS go to author if
     editor feels they are helpful; many rejects are accepted
     after revision.
Manuscript Disposition: Receipt of MS acknowledged; 3-4
     months required for decision; "blind" refereeing; rejected
     MS returned (one copy); critique to author; 25-30% sub-
     mitted MSS accepted; 28-30 MSS published/yr.; 6-9
     months from acceptance to publication; generally first ac-
     cepted, first published.
Style Requirements: Consult journal and APA Publication

Manual; preferred length 1500 to 3000 words; avoid both "padding" and omission of essential content; 3 copies of MS; abstract of approximately 175 words; be parsimonious in use of tables, as they are costly to set; development of ideas should be clear and logical, without overlap; avoid jargon or stilted construction; avoid footnotes; author's name, position, title and place of employment should appear only on a cover page, to insure "blind" reviewing.

Payments: None to or by author.

Reprints: Copies of journal issue may be provided; reprints available by purchase.

98 MERRILL-PALMER QUARTERLY (1954) of Behavior and Development

Martin L. Hoffman, Department of Psychology, University of Michigan, Ann Arbor, MI

Publisher & Copyright: The Merrill-Palmer Institute, 71 East Ferry Ave., Detroit, MI 48202

Subscriptions: Instit. & Indiv. $11/yr. Indiv. member $8.50/yr. Quarterly. Ca. 2200. 80 pages/issue.

Description: "Major purpose is to stimulate the growth of ideas in the various disciplines bearing on human development. To this end the Quarterly welcomes conceptual analyses of problems under investigation, results of exploratory studies in new areas, and case material illustrative of general principles, as well as completed research reports. Theoretical papers and critical reviews are particularly welcome. Articles having practical value, when documented with data support or sound theoretical analyses are also seen as contributing to the purposes of the journal."

Article Content: Socialization in childhood or adolescence; infant development; cognitive development including effects of intervention; effects of family and social structure on socialization.

Typical Disciplines: Mostly psychology; also education, sociology, and social work.

Intended Audience: University faculty; researchers; administrators; practitioners; students in psychology and education.

Special Features: Research reports; theoretical articles; book reviews; literature reviews; special theme for some issues; bi-annual index.

Acceptance/Rejection Criteria: Significance of paper (important topic, major contribution); quality of research and data analysis (how well was research designed and how competently executed); quality of presentation (well-organized and well-written, length appropriate to content); in evaluating MSS, the level of development of the topical field to which the paper contributes is also taken into consideration. For theoretical contributions, critical reviews, syntheses of literature, and case studies special attention is given to originality, relevance to important issues, inner consistency, and congruence with known facts.

Acceptance/Rejection Procedures: Each MS is reviewed by two specialists in the field; publication decision is based on these reviews; major disagreements decided by a third reviewer or by the editor.

Manuscript Disposition: Receipt of MS acknowledged; 4-8 weeks required for decision; "blind" refereeing; rejected MS returned; critique to author; 20-25% submitted MSS accepted; 25-30 MSS published/yr.; 8-12 months from acceptance to publication; first accepted, first published.

Style Requirements: APA Publication Manual; preferred length 10-25 pages, double spaced; no minimum length, 50 pages maximum length; 2 copies of MS; abstract not required.

Payment: None to author; author not charged except for occasional articles having excessive tabular or graphic material.

Reprints: 50 free (this practice may be eliminated in the future); charge for additional nominal and varies with amount ordered.

99 MULTIVARIATE BEHAVIORAL RESEARCH (1966)

Dr. Benjamin Fruchter, Dept. of Educational Psychology, University of Texas, Austin, TX 78712
Publisher & Copyright: Society of Multivariate Experimental Psychology.
Subscriptions: Instit. $20/yr. Indiv. $12.50/yr. Students, $7.50/yr. (Certified by Dept. Chairman or major professor.) Quarterly. Ca. 850. 128 pages/issue. Address Business Manager, Multivariate Behavioral Research, Texas Christian University, Fort Worth, TX 76129

Description: "Journal published substantive, methodological,

and theoretical articles. Substantive articles report results of behavioral research employing multivariate methods. Methodological articles present new multivariate
mathematico-statistical procedures or definitive critical
contributions of methodological or substantive interest.
Theoretical articles may convey new insight into the historical development of multivariate scientific approaches,
formulate meta-theoretical principles governing program-
matic research, or provide new conceptual multivariate
models for researchable systems. "

Typical Disciplines: Psychology; education; related behavioral
sciences.

Intended Audience: Teachers; researchers; students.

Special Features: Research reports; theoretical articles; abstract for each article; annual index; brief reports of
new findings, new equations or new lines of research;
monographs (at irregular intervals).

Acceptance/Rejection Criteria: Appropriateness; quality of
contribution; required format; clarity and conciseness.

Acceptance/Rejection Procedures: Reviewed by two consulting editors; editor makes final decision.

Manuscript Disposition: Receipt of MS acknowledged; 8 weeks
required for decision; rejected MS returned; critique to
author; 50% submitted MSS accepted; 40 MSS published/
yr.; 12 months from acceptance to publication; first accepted, first published.

Style Requirements: APA Publication Manual and journal;
preferred length 35 pages, maximum 65 pages, double
spaced; longer MSS may be published as monographs; 3
copies of MS; abstract of 120 words required; equations
should be triple-spaced and numbered in square brackets
on the left.

Payment: None to author; charges to contributors per printed
page vary between $14 and $21, according to the type of
copy involved. Formulas, tables and other copy requiring special composition cost more than straight copy.
Page charges for articles cover only the cost of composition. For unsponsored publications running ten printed
pages or less, the journal charges page costs up to a
maximum of about $90. For monographs the author pays
the full costs for printing and binding. All charges must
be paid before the paper is set in type.

Reprints: Rates supplied at time author receives information
about the page cost.

100 NEW VOICES IN EDUCATION (1970) A graduate student journal

Editor, New Voices in Education, 2456 Norman Hall, University of Florida, Gainesville, FL 32601
Publisher: New Voices in Education
Subscriptions: Instit. & Indiv. $5/yr. Student $2/yr. Contributing membership $15/yr. Sustaining membership $25/yr. Quarterly. Ca. 600. 32 pages/issue.

Description: "Purpose to provide a seminar in print wherein graduate students may publish their ideas on all aspects of education. It is a community of educators and caring people that we seek."
Article Content: Humanism vs. behaviorism; free schools; anthropology in education; alternative education; the black experience in education; counselor education; concept of the helper; group dynamics in the classroom.
Typical Disciplines: Psychological foundations of education; psychology; counselor education; childhood and secondary education.
Intended Audience: Beginning and advanced graduate students; practitioners.
Special Features: Theoretical articles; book reviews; editorials; hortatory or polemical articles; special theme each issue.

Acceptance/Rejection Criteria: MSS must be written by students--undergraduate or graduate.
Acceptance/Rejection Procedures: No formal procedures, merely intensive perusal of submitted MSS and active soliciting of others.
Manuscript Disposition: Receipt of MS acknowledged; 6 months required for decision; rejected MS returned; 20% submitted MSS accepted; 30 MSS published/yr.; 3-6 months from acceptance to publication.
Style Requirements: No formal statement; preferred length 8-10 pages double spaced or 2000-2500 words; minimum length 3 pages, or 800 words; maximum length 20 pages or 5000 words; 2 copies of MS; no abstract required.
Payment: None to or by author.
Reprints: Not available.

101 NEW YORK UNIVERSITY EDUCATION QUARTERLY (1969)

Lila S. Rosenblum, (New York University) 51 Press Building,

32 Washington Square, New York, NY 10003
<u>Publisher & Copyright:</u> New York University School of Education.
<u>Subscriptions:</u> Price not applicable. Quarterly. Ca. 52,000.
32 pages/issue.

<u>Description:</u> "Devoted to the examination of important issues in education."
<u>Article Content:</u> Behavior research; counseling; administration; allied health areas; content areas like music, religion, social studies, health education.
<u>Typical Disciplines:</u> Educational psychology; administration; teacher education; history and philosophy of education; higher education.
<u>Intended Audience:</u> Professional persons concerned with education at all levels; alumni and faculty of the New York University School of Education; deans and libraries at other schools of education and chairmen of undergraduate departments of education; key professional associations; superintendents of schools in large cities; and municipal, state, and federal officials; audience nationwide; 75% hold M.A., 10% Ph.D.
<u>Special Features:</u> Research reports; theoretical articles; book reviews; letters to the editor; hortatory or polemical articles.

<u>Acceptance/Rejection Criteria:</u> Articles should be written for the generalist in education as well as for the specialist; terms not in common use require definition or illustration; experimental results should be presented in a way that is understandable to the larger audience; desirable that papers be written in a narrative style, in as lively a manner as subject permits; material should be documented and research cited whenever possible.
<u>Acceptance/Rejection Procedures:</u> All MSS, whether or not they have been solicited, will be subject to review by at least three members of the Editorial Board and/or outside experts. Reviewers are asked to judge overall soundness of the MS and its significance for the Quarterly audience--generalist and specialist alike. They are also requested to make constructive suggestions relating to specific points that in their opinion should be added, deleted, or clarified in order to strengthen the presentation.
<u>Manuscript Disposition:</u> Receipt of MS acknowledged; 4-6 months required for decision; "blind" refereeing; rejected MS returned; critique to author; 70% submitted MSS accepted; 12-15 MSS published/yr.; 6 months from accep-

tance to publication; usually first accepted, first published.

Style Requirements: Guide available from editors; preferred
length between 3000 and 5000 words, or 12 to 20 pages;
2 copies of MS; abstract not required; tone and level on
the order of that found in Scientific American; when original findings are presented, include only short tables in
the body of the text; use reference numbers in paren-
theses at appropriate point in text and list full bibliographic information numerically in an appended section
labeled "Notes;" subheads will be used every 500 or so
words, and authors may include subheads or leave this
to the editor's discretion; see also A Manual of Style,
University of Chicago.

Payment: None to or by author.

Reprints: Reprints of particular articles are not available.
Usually there are enough magazines available to fill an
author's requests.

102 PEABODY JOURNAL OF EDUCATION (1923)

Ralph E. Kirkman, Peabody College, Box 41, Nashville, TN
37203

Publisher & Copyright: George Peabody College for Teachers

Subscriptions: Instit. $8/yr. Indiv. $6/yr. Quarterly.
Ca. 2600. 88 pages/issue. Address subscription correspondence to Executive Secretary.

Description: "Is interdisciplinary and is designed to foster
the professional development and enrichment of teachers,
administrators, and other leaders in education. Its basic
goal is to provide a medium for the publication of relevant educational research and essays."

Article Content: A variety of scholarly articles, some of
which report significant educational research and others
which express in provocative and exciting language new
directions which should be attempted in education. Also
essays dealing with significant issues in education. All
levels of the educational process included.

Intended Audience: Teachers; administrators; researchers;
practitioners; students.

Special Features: Special theme for each issue plus small
section concerned with educational matters not directly
related to the basic theme of the issue; book reviews and
on occasion book notes; research reports; theoretical articles; editorials; annual index; 50-year cumulative index
in progress; advertising.

Acceptance/Rejection Criteria: Appropriateness of contents; quality of ideas or research (originality, importance, logic of thought); the writing itself (organization, clarity, interest, grammar, style); a majority of MSS are solicited.

Acceptance/Rejection Procedures: MSS are reviewed by at least three members of the Editorial Board. Editor reads reviews and makes final decision.

Manuscript Disposition: Receipt of MS acknowledged; 35 days required for decision; "blind" refereeing; rejected MS returned if stamped self-addressed envelope is supplied; 40 MSS published/yr.; 3-9 months from acceptance to publication.

Style Requirements: See journal, also MLA Style Sheet, second edition; preferred length 6-10 pages double spaced; 3 copies of MS; abstract not required; author's name and institutional association should be indicated on a separate sheet of paper rather than on the MS; footnotes should be placed on a separate page at the end of each MS; unsolicited contributions should be accompanied by a stamped self-addressed envelope.

Payment: None to or by author.

Reprints: 6 free copies of issue; reprints available at publication cost only.

103 PERCEPTUAL AND MOTOR SKILLS (1948)

R. B. Ammons and C. H. Ammons (University of Montana)
    P.O. Box 1441, Missoula, MT 59801

Publisher & Copyright: Perceptual and Motor Skills, P.O. Box 1441

Subscriptions: Indiv. & Instit. $56/yr. Bimonthly. Ca. 2000. 340 pages/issue.

Description: "Purpose is to encourage scientific originality and creativity. Material of the following kinds is carried: experimental or theoretical articles dealing with perception or motor skills, especially as affected by experience; articles on general methodology; new material listing & reviews."

Intended Audience: People in the following fields: psychology; anthropology; physical education; physical therapy; orthopedics; time and motion.

Special Features: Research reports; theoretical articles; book reviews; letters to the editor; editorials; literature reviews; abstract for each article; annual index; policy to

file raw data with the American Society for Information
Science.

Acceptance/Rejection Criteria: Reasonable question; good design; well organized; documentation. Attempt made to
balance critical editing by specific suggestions as to
changes and to make the approach interdisciplinary.

Acceptance/Rejection Procedures: MS reviewed by 3 to 15
people, depending on difficulty; criticisms and suggestions
summarized; cooperation of author elicited; MS revised
or author encouraged to withdraw.

Manuscript Disposition: Receipt of MS acknowledged; 4 to 6
weeks required for decision; author may nominate referees and have "blind" refereeing if so desires; rejected
MS returned; critique to author; 40% submitted MSS accepted; 600 MSS published/yr.; 4 to 6 weeks from acceptance to publication; MSS published in order of receipt of
proofs from authors.

Payment: None to author.

Reprints: For regular articles and monograph supplements
the reprint charge is approximately $20 per page in mul-
tiples of 4 pages for 200 copies.

104 PERSONNEL & GUIDANCE JOURNAL
formerly NVGA Bulletin; Vocational Guidance Magazine;
Occupations

Leo Goldman, American Personnel & Guidance Association,
1607 New Hampshire Avenue N.W., Washington, D.C.
20009

Publisher & Copyright: American Personnel & Guidance Association.

Subscriptions: Instit. & Indiv. non-member $20/yr. Mem-
bership in APGA includes a subscription to journal.
Monthly Sept. to June. Ca. 38,000. 80 pages/issue.

Description: "The official journal of the American Personnel
& Guidance Association. Its purpose is to foster the professional practice of guidance, counseling, and student
personnel work in schools, colleges, vocational counseling centers, rehabilitation agencies, and employment
agencies."

Intended Audience: Counselors and personnel workers at all
educational levels from kindergarten to higher education,
in community agencies, and in government, business, and
industry; students in education and psychology.

Special Features: Research reports (rare); theoretical articles; book reviews; letters to the editor; editorials; hortatory or polemical articles; literature reviews; dialogues; poems; brief descriptions of new practices and
programs; abstract for each article; annual index; available on microfilm; advertising.

Acceptance/Rejection Criteria: Especially welcome are articles dealing with new techniques or innovative practices
and programs; discussions of current professional and
scientific issues; scholarly commentaries on APGA as an
association, and its role in society; critical integrations
of published research; and research reports of unusual
significance to practitioners. Dialogues, poems, and
brief descriptions of new practices and programs will
also be considered. All material should aim to communicate ideas clearly and interestingly to a readership composed mainly of practitioners. Relevance, quality of
ideas, and quality of writing are important.

Acceptance/Rejection Procedure: Editor reads all MSS first,
immediately rejects about half as either not appropriate
or below standards. Remaining MSS then reviewed anonymously by 2 members of Editorial Board. Editor makes
final decision.

Manuscript Disposition: Receipt of MS acknowledged; 2-3
months required for decision; "blind" refereeing; rejected
MS returned (one copy kept); critique to author; 20% submitted MSS accepted; 100 MSS published/yr.; 5 months
from acceptance to publication; generally first accepted,
first published.

Style Requirements: Consult journal; MS should not exceed
3500 words (approximately 13 pages of double-spaced
typewritten copy including references, tables, and figures)
nor should it be less than 2000 words; "In the Field" articles should not exceed 2500 words; submit original and
2 copies; double-space all copy; avoid footnotes; place
authors' names, positions, titles, place of employment,
and mailing addresses on cover page only, so MSS may
be reviewed anonymously; abstract of not more than 100
words with each copy of MS (on separate page).

Payment: None to or by author for publication.

Reprints: Senior author receives 10 copies of journal issue
(poetry 5 copies); reprints available at charge.

105 PERSONNEL PSYCHOLOGY (1948) A Journal of Applied
Research

Milton D. Hakel, Department of Psychology, Ohio State University, 1945 N. High St., Columbus, OH 43210
Publisher & Copyright: Personnel Psychology, Inc., P.O. Box 6965 College Station, Durham, N.C. 27708
Subscriptions: Instit. & Indiv. $15/yr. Quarterly. 200 pages/issue.

Description: "Purpose to report research methods, research results, or their application to the solution of personnel problems in business, industry and government."
Article Content: Personnel training, selection, classification and placement; morale; job satisfaction; organizational structure; job analysis and structure.
Typical Disciplines: Industrial/organizational psychology; social psychology; statistics; demography; business administration.
Intended Audience: Dual audience of the operating personnel official and personnel technician; teachers; researchers; students.
Special Features: Research reports; theoretical articles; book reviews; abstract for each article; annual index; literature reviews.

Acceptance/Rejection Criteria: Technical soundness (adequately designed, well controlled research); readability; practicality; priority to papers whose implications are for immediate and general problems.
Acceptance/Rejection Procedures: MSS reviewed by Editorial Board and Editor.
Manuscript Disposition: Receipt of MS acknowledged; 1 month required for decision; rejected MS returned; critique to author; 15% submitted MSS accepted; 50 MSS published/yr.; 18 months from acceptance to publication; usually first accepted, first published; authors can hasten publication by paying extra-page costs.
Style Requirements: APA Publication Manual and journal; preferred length 4000 words; 3 copies of MS; abstract required; journal titles not abbreviated; tables and footnotes on separate pages from text.
Payment: None to author; author pays $30 per page of running text and $40 per page of tables, figures, and formulas for publication.
Reprints: Available for charge.

106 PHI DELTA KAPPAN (1915)

Stanley M. Elam, Phi Delta Kappa, 8th & Union Sts., Bloom-

ington, IN 47401
Publisher & Copyright: Phi Delta Kappa
Subscriptions: Instit. & Indiv. $8/yr. Included in dues for
members of Phi Delta Kappa. Monthly September-June.
Ca. 100,000. 72 pages/issue.

Description: "To promote leadership in education--from
teaching to administration and policy."
Article Content: All related to education policy and processes.
Intended Audience: Teachers; teacher educators; school administrators; university professors and doctoral students;
education researchers; state and federal education agency
personnel.
Special Features: Research reports; theoretical articles; book
reviews; letters to the editor; editorials; literature reviews; special theme for some issues; annual index; available on microform; advertising.

Acceptance/Rejection Criteria: Significance; readability; whatever is uniquely informative or inspiring, whatever will
contribute to research, service, and leadership, whatever
says something that Kappans ought to know about, expressed in a way that makes the reader hungry for more,
is what magazine is looking for.
Acceptance/Rejection Procedures: MSS reviewed by editors
and editorial consultants; attempt made to balance selections, including some that will appeal to younger readers
and some to more mature; some of a research nature,
some of an anecdotal; some in a serious vein, some
light; some incontrovertibly factual, some admittedly controversial.
Manuscript Disposition: Receipt of MS acknowledged; 2
months required for decision; "blind" refereeing, rejected
MS returned; critique to author; less than 10% of unsolicited MSS accepted; 150 MSS published/yr.; 2 months to
2 years from acceptance to publication.
Style Requirements: Best guide is reading the magazine itself; preferred length 1500 to 3500 words; 2 copies of
MS; no abstract.
Payment: Usually none to or by author; occasional honorari-
um for solicited material.
Reprints: 10 free; reprints available in units of 100.

107 PROFESSIONAL PSYCHOLOGY (1959)

Donald K. Freedheim, Department of Psychology, Case

Western Reserve University, Cleveland, OH 44106
Publisher & Copyright: American Psychological Association,
1200 17th Street N. W. , Washington, D. C. 20036
Subscriptions: Instit. & Indiv. $12/yr. Quarterly. Ca.
8000. 125 pages/issue. Subscriptions available on
calendar year basis only.

Description: "Covers the broad range of psychological specialties devoted to the promotion of human welfare. Psychological principles and skills are applied in a wide
variety of settings: clinics, hospitals, schools, industry,
rehabilitation institutions, community agencies, government, and independent practice. Whatever the context in
which they work, psychologists share common problems
and challenges: ethical issues, educational preparation;
continuing education, social action roles, and professional obligations, opportunities, and benefits. "
Article Content: Applications of research; standards of practice; interprofessional relations; innovative approaches to
training and to the delivery of services; training, practice, and teaching and their relationship to issues of human welfare.
Intended Audience: Students; educators; researchers; administrators; particularly practitioners; those whose work involves meeting human needs on an individual, group, or
community basis.
Special Features: Reports on organizational activities at the
national, state, and local levels, as well as on international developments; forum for the exchange of opinions;
special student forum; review section covering professional books, leisure reading, films, and the arts; historical
references in psychology; innovations in training; bibliographies; letters to the editor; editorials; abstract for
each article and biographical sketch of author; annual index; advertising.

Acceptance/Rejection Criteria: Invites original articles on
both theory and techniques which will enhance knowledge
and improve the effectiveness of psychologists; makes significant contribution; clear and concise; conforms to APA
style requirements.
Manuscript Disposition: Receipt of MS acknowledged; 2
months required for decision; MS reviewed by 2 referees;
rejected MS returned; critique to author; 35% submitted
MSS accepted; 50 MSS published/yr.; 1 year from acceptance to publication.
Style Requirements: APA Publication Manual or journal;

preferred length 8-12 pages, double spaced; maximum length 20 pages; 2 copies of MS; abstract of approximately 150 words required.

Payment: None to or by author.

Reprints: Available at charge depending on length of article.

108 PSYCHOLOGICAL BULLETIN (1905)

James Deese, Gilmer Hall, Department of Psychology, University of Virginia, Charlottesville, VA 22901

Publisher & Copyright: American Psychological Association, 1200 17th Street N.W., Washington, D.C. 20036

Subscriptions: Inst. & Indiv. $24/yr. Monthly. Ca. 8000. 75 pages/issue. Subscriptions available on calendar year basis only.

Description: "Concerned with research reviews and methodological contributions in the field of psychology. One of its principal functions is to publish critical, evaluative summaries of research. The methodological articles are directed toward people who might or do make practical use of such information, and are intended to bridge the gap between the technical statistician and the typical research psychologist."

Article Content: Articles feature the application of new methodology as well as the creative application of more familiar methodology.

Typical Disciplines: Psychology; education; physiology; sociology; statistics.

Intended Audience: Teachers; researchers; administrators; practitioners; students.

Special Features: Literature reviews.

Acceptance/Rejection Criteria: Publishes original research only when these are used to illustrate some methodological problem or issue. Methodological issues should be aimed at the solution of some particular research problem in psychology, but issues should be of sufficient breadth to interest a wide readership among psychologists. Articles of a more specialized nature are not accepted. Also, original theoretical articles are not accepted.

Acceptance/Rejection Procedures: Papers are rejected by the Editor if they do not meet policy. Otherwise, all MSS are reviewed by one or more consultants and the final decision made by the Editor.

Manuscript Disposition: Receipt of MS acknowledged; 40 days

required for decision; "blind" refereeing; rejected MS returned; critique to author; 10% submitted MSS accepted;
50 MSS published/yr.; 11 months from acceptance to publication; first accepted, first published.
Style Requirements: APA Publication Manual, journal; maximum length 50 pages, double spaced; 2 copies of MS;
include a cover sheet with each copy giving title of MS,
author's name, institutional affiliation, date; first page
should include title of article and date, but omit author's
name and affiliation; MS should contain no clues to author's identity; give full journal titles, do not abbreviate.
Payment: None to or by author.
Reprints: Available at charge when return galley proofs.

109 THE PSYCHOLOGICAL RECORD (1937)

Irvin S. Wolf, Denison University, Granville, OH 43023
Publisher & Copyright: Denison University
Subscriptions: Instit. $10/yr. Indiv. $6/yr. Student $4/
yr. Quarterly. Ca. 1900. 150 pages/issue

Description: "Publishes experimental and theoretical papers
in the psychological area and commentary on current
developments in psychology. A journal of general interest in the field of psychology."
Intended Audience: All professionals and students in psychology.
Special Features: Research reports; theoretical articles; book
reviews; literature reviews; abstract for each article;
annual index; available on microform.

Acceptance/Rejection Criteria: Favors new approaches to the
study of behavior and critiques of existing approaches and
methods.
Acceptance/Rejection Procedures: Receipt of MS acknowledged;
1 to 3 months required for decision; "blind" refereeing;
rejected MS returned; critique to author; 40% submitted
MSS accepted; 50-60 MSS published/yr.; 1-2 months from
acceptance to publication.
Style Requirements: APA Publication Manual and journal;
preferred length 6 to 18 pages, double spaced; no minimum, maximum length; 2 copies of MS; abstract required.
Payment: None to author; authors assessed a publication
charge of approximately $12/pg and $8/each for figures
and tables.
Reprints: Available at charge (approximately $15/100, $30/
300).

110 PSYCHOLOGICAL REPORTS (1955)

R. B. Ammons and C. H. Ammons (University of Montana)
P. O. Box 1441, Missoula, MT 59801
Publisher & Copyright: Psychological Record, P. O. Box
1441, Missoula, MT 59801
Subscriptions: $56/yr. Bimonthly. Ca. 2000. 340 pages/issue.

Description: "Purpose is to encourage scientific originality
and creativity in the field of general psychology for persons who are first psychologists, then specialists."
Article Content: Entire range of psychology and then some.
Intended Audience: Psychologists; students.
Special Features: Experimental, theoretical, and speculative
articles; special reviews; listing of new books and other
material received; controversial material of scientific
merit; letters to the editor; editorials; abstract for each
article; annual index; policy to file raw data with the
American Society for Information Science.

Acceptance/Rejection Criteria: Reasonable question; good design; well organized; documentation; attempt made to balance critical editing by specific standards.
Acceptance/Rejection Procedures: Review by 3 to 15 persons,
depending on difficulty; criticism and suggestions summarized; cooperation of author elicited; MSS revised or
author encouraged to withdraw.
Manuscript Disposition: Receipt of MS acknowledged; 4 to
6 weeks required for decision; author may nominate
referee and have "blind" refereeing if desires; rejected
MS returned; critique to author; 40% submitted MSS accepted; 600 MSS published/yr.; 1 month to 6 weeks from
acceptance to publication; MSS published in order of receipt of proof from authors.
Style Requirements: APA Publication Manual and journal; no
preferred length; 2 copies of MS; abstract required.
Payment: None to author.
Reprints: For regular articles and monograph supplements
reprint charge is $20/page in multiples of 4 pages for
200 copies.

111 PSYCHOLOGICAL REVIEW (1894)

Dr. George Mandler, Department of Psychology, University
of California, San Diego, La Jolla, CA 92037
Publisher & Copyright: American Psychological Association,

1200 17th Street N.W., Washington, D.C. 20036
<u>Subscriptions</u>: Instit. & Indiv. $15/yr. Available on Jan.-
Dec. basis only. Bimonthly. Ca. 7000. 94 pages/
issue.

<u>Description</u>: "Devoted to articles of theoretical significance
to any area of scientific endeavor in psychology. Contains original articles which propose theoretical ideas
and developments, and offers critical discussions of theoretical issues."
<u>Article Content</u>: Any area of psychology, from personality,
social to learning, perception, cognition, psychophysics;
memory; speech perception; food intake; learning sets;
drive and incentive; conceptual behavior; cognitive inter-
actions; pastural sets; depth perceptions.
<u>Typical Disciplines</u>: Psychology; sociology; philosophy; an-
thropology; neurosciences.
<u>Intended Audience</u>: Teachers; researchers; students.
<u>Special Features</u>: Theoretical articles and notes; letters to
the Editor; abstract for each article; annual index; advertising.

<u>Acceptance/Rejection Criteria</u>: Articles must clearly be
theoretical contributions to the field; methodological and
statistical articles, and ordinarily original reports of
research or reviews of literature are not appropriate;
quality.
<u>Acceptance/Rejection Procedures</u>: MSS are evaluated ini-
tially by editor or associate editor who may reject out-
right, usually on basis of appropriateness; approximately
67% of all MSS submitted are evaluated by referees.
<u>Manuscript Disposition</u>: Receipt of MS acknowledged; 4 weeks
required for decision; "blind" refereeing; rejected MS returned; critique to author; 18% submitted MSS accepted;
50 MSS published/yr.; 7 months from acceptance to publication; first accepted, first published.
<u>Style Requirements</u>: APA Publication Manual and journal;
preferred length of MS 30-45 pages, double spaced;
normally MSS not over 7500 words; 3 copies of MS; abstract of 100-120 words required.
<u>Payment</u>: None to or by author.
<u>Reprints</u>: Available at charge.

112 PSYCHOLOGY IN THE SCHOOLS (1963)

Gerald B. Fuller, Department of Psychology, Sloan Hall,

Central Michigan University, Mt. Pleasant, MI 48858
Publisher & Copyright: Clinical Psychology Press, 4 Conant
Square, Brandon, VT 05733
Subscriptions: Instit. & Indiv. $20/yr. Student $8/yr.
Quarterly. Ca. 2800. 120 pages/issue.

Description: "Devoted to research, opinion, and practice.
Deals with theoretical and other problems of the school
psychologist to those directed to the teacher, counselor,
administrator and other personnel workers in schools
and colleges, public and private organizations. Preference given to MSS that clearly describe implications for
the practitioner in the schools. "
Article Content: Educational practices & problems; evaluation
and assessment; strategies in behavioral change.
Intended Audience: Teachers; researchers; administrators;
practitioners; graduate students in psychology and education.
Special Features: Research reports; theoretical articles;
book reviews; literature reviews; editorials; test reviews.

Acceptance/Rejection Criteria: Psychological value; meth-
odological competence; theoretical significance; presentation quality; practical significance.
Acceptance/Rejection Procedures: Two reviewers for each
MS, plus editor; author always given reasons as to why
MS rejected.
Manuscript Disposition: Receipt of MS acknowledged; one
month required for decision; "blind" refereeing; rejected
MS returned; critique to author; 45% submitted MSS accepted; 80 to 100 MSS published/yr.; 9 months from acceptance to publication.
Style Requirements: APA Publication Manual and journal;
preferred length 10 to 12 pages, double spaced; minimum
length 1 page, maximum 20 pages; 3 copies of MS; abstract required.
Payment: None to author; authors are assessed a publication
charge per printed page and table.

113 PSYCHOMETRIKA (1936)

Bert F. Green, Dept. of Psychology, Johns Hopkins Univer-
sity, Charles at 34th St., Baltimore, MD 21218
Publisher & Copyright: Psychometric Society.
Subscriptions: Instit. $20/yr. Indiv. non-member $20/yr.
Indiv. member $10/yr. Student member $5/yr. Sub-

scriptions start in March and cover calendar year. Subscriptions from Howard Wainer, Treasurer, Psychometric
Society, Department of Psychology, University of Chicago,
5848 University Avenue, Chicago, IL 60637. Quarterly.
Ca. 2500. 150 pages/issue.

Description: "A journal devoted to the development of psychology as a quantitative rational science."
Article Content: The development of quantitative models for
 psychological phenomena (priority); general theoretical
 articles on quantitative methodology in the social, behavioral, and biological sciences; new mathematical and
 statistical techniques for the evaluation of psychological
 data; aids in the application of statistical techniques such
 as nomographs, tables, algorithms, and apparatus; reviews or reports of significant empirical studies involving
 new or particularly interesting uses of quantitative techniques.
Typical Disciplines: Psychology; statistics; education.
Intended Audience: Advanced graduate students & specialists;
 teachers; researchers.
Special Features: Theoretical articles; book reviews; letters
 to the editor; monographs; Psychometric Society minutes
 and other information; abstract for each article; annual
 index.

Acceptance/Rejection Criteria: Manuscripts must be appropriate, original, correct, clear, and brief.
Acceptance/Rejection Process: All manuscripts are received
 by the Managing Editor. He, or one of the associate
 editors, solicits reviews from two or three editorial consultants and recommends action. The author receives
 pertinent portions of the reviews. The manuscript may
 be accepted, in which case the author may wish to make
 small revisions suggested by the consultants. A promis-
 ing manuscript that seems to require substantial revision
 is rejected with encouragement to resubmit. Unpromis-
 ing or inappropriate manuscripts are rejected. Manuscripts are not accepted conditional upon certain alterations. A revised and resubmitted manuscript is reevalu-
 ated.
Manuscript Disposition: Receipt of MS acknowledged; 6
 months required for decision; "blind" refereeing; one copy
 of rejected MS returned; critique to author; 30% submitted
 MSS accepted; 30 MSS published/yr.; 9 months from acceptance to publication; MSS published in order of receipt
 of final revised form of MS, after acceptance.

<u>Style Requirements</u>: APA Publication Manual and journal;
preferred length 10-25 pages, double spaced; monograph
supplement available for very long MSS; 4 copies of MS;
4 copies of abstract of no more than 100 words; 4 copies
of tables; separate sheet giving title, author's name and
professional connection should be included; author's name
or professional connection should not appear elsewhere,
to insure "blind" refereeing.

<u>Payment</u>: None to or by author.

<u>Reprints</u>: 100 free; additional charge about $4 plus $1.60/2
pages/100 copies.

114 REPRESENTATIVE RESEARCH IN SOCIAL PSYCHOLOGY (1970)

<u>Editor</u>: Graduate students in social psychology at the Univer-
sity of North Carolina at Chapel Hill.

<u>Editorial Address</u>: Department of Psychology, Davie Hall,
University of North Carolina, Chapel Hill, NC 27514
(Address all correspondence to Editorial Address)

<u>Copyright</u>: Representative Research in Social Psychology.

<u>Subscriptions</u>: Instit. $10/yr. Indiv. $4/yr. Issued twice
a year. Ca. 350. 80 pages/issue.

<u>Description</u>: "Purpose is promotion of methodological im-
provement in the field and replications of important work.
Hopes to establish a priority for ascertaining the reliability of psychological phenomena and for disseminating
a less biased sample of methodologically sound findings
than is presently available."

<u>Article Content</u>: General articles in social psychology, in-
cluding experimental research, field research, theoretical
articles, methodological notes, and positive and negative
replications.

<u>Intended Audience</u>: Anyone interested in social psychology.

<u>Special Features</u>: Theoretical articles; methodological notes;
editorials; abstract for each article; annual index; limited
advertising.

<u>Acceptance/Rejection Criteria</u>: Adequacy of design and re-
search methods; relevance to theoretical issues; like to
receive replications whether positive or negative.

<u>Acceptance/Rejection Procedures</u>: Some articles solicited;
associate editors review MSS with review staff and outside reviewers in special areas of interest and make decision.

Manuscript Disposition: 2-3 months required for decision; "blind" refereeing; rejected MS returned; critique to author; 1 out of 6 submitted MSS accepted; 20 MSS published/yr.; 2-3 months from acceptance to publication; first accepted, first published.

Style Requirements: APA Publication Manual; preferred length 20 pages, double spaced, or less; 2 copies of MS; abstract of up to 125 words required; when MS is over 20 pages, a 1000-2000 word summary is also needed.

Payment: None to or by author.

Reprints: Charge for additional reprints based on sliding scale. Journal notifies author.

115 RESEARCH IN HIGHER EDUCATION (1973)

Charles F. Elton, College of Education, Department of Higher Education, University of Kentucky, Lexington, KY 40506

Publisher & Copyright: APS Publications, Inc., 150 Fifth Ave., New York 10011

Subscriptions: Instit. $20/yr. Indiv. $12/yr. Quarterly. 100 pages/issue.

Description: "The journal will publish quantitative studies that contribute to an increased understanding of an institution or that allow comparison between institutions, that aid faculty and administrators in making more informed decisions about current or future operations, and that improve the efficiency or effectiveness of their institution."

Article Content: Administration and faculty; curriculum and instruction; student characteristics; alumni assessment; recruitment and admissions; prediction and student academic performance; campus climate; retention, attribution and transfer.

Intended Audience: Institutional researchers and planners; faculty; college and university administrators; student personnel specialists and behavioral scientists; beginning graduate students in psychology and education.

Special Features: Research reports; brief notes of a methodological nature.

Acceptance/Rejection Criteria: Significance in contributing new knowledge; technical adequacy; appropriateness for Research in Higher Education; clarity of presentation.

Acceptance/Rejection Procedures: MS sent to 2 consulting

editors for review. If both agree, their decision becomes the editorial decision. If they disagree, the editor casts the deciding vote.

Manuscript Disposition: Receipt of MS acknowledged; 30 days required for decision; "blind" refereeing; rejected MS returned; critique to author; 60% submitted MSS accepted; 35-40 MSS published/yr.; first accepted, first published.

Style Requirements: APA Publication Manual; preferred length 20 pages, double spaced; no minimum, maximum length; 2 copies of MS required; each page of MS should be numbered; first page should contain the article title, author's name, affiliation and address to which correspondence should be sent; for "blind" refereeing authors should not place their name elsewhere on MS; second page should contain abstract of 100 to 120 words.

Payment: None to author; charge will be made for alterations in galley proofs in excess of 10% of the charge of composition.

Reprints: Order form sent with galley proofs.

116 REVIEW OF EDUCATIONAL RESEARCH

Samuel Messick, Box 2604, Educational Testing Service, Princeton, NJ 08546

Publisher & Copyright: American Educational Research Association, 1126 16th St., N.W., Washington, D.C. 20036

Subscriptions: $10/yr., $18/2 yrs. AERA members receive as part of membership. Quarterly. 130 pages/issue.

Description: "Publishes critical, integrative reviews of research literature bearing on education. Includes reviews and interpretations of substantive and methodological issues."

Acceptance/Rejection Criteria: All MSS submitted will be considered. There is no restriction on topics reviewed.

Style Requirements: APA Publication Manual; no restrictions on page length; 3 copies of MS; abstract not required.

117 SMALL GROUP BEHAVIOR (1970)
formerly, Comparative Group Studies

William Fawcett Hill (California State Polytechnic Univ.)

Publisher & Copyright: Sage Publications, Inc., 275 So. Beverly Drive, Beverly Hills, CA 90212 (Send all

correspondence to this address).
Subscriptions: Instit. $18/yr. Indiv. $10/yr. Student $9/
yr. Quarterly. 128 pages/issue.

Description: "Is an international and interdisciplinary journal
presenting research and theory about all types of small
groups, including but not limited to, therapy and treatment groups. Its long-term goal is to encourage the development of a comparative social science of group work."
Typical Disciplines: Psychology; sociology; social work; organization & management.
Intended Audience: Researchers; administrators; practitioners;
students; all group work professionals.
Special Features: Research reports; theoretical articles;
book reviews; letters to the editor; literature reviews;
special theme for some issues; up-to-date bibliographic
listings; news of significant professional activities such
as meetings and research centers; annual index; advertising.

Acceptance/Rejection Procedures: Appropriate MSS sent to
two members of the journal's editorial advisory board.
Judgments are pooled and used by the editor in making
final decisions.
Manuscript Disposition: Receipt of MS acknowledged; 8-12
weeks required for decision; "blind" refereeing; rejected
MS returned; 20-25% submitted MSS accepted; 25-30 MSS
published/yr.; 6-9 months from acceptance to publication; first accepted, first published.
Style Requirements: Available upon request from editor or
publisher; preferred length of MS 25-30 pages, double
spaced; 2 copies of MS; abstract not required.
Payment: None to or by author.
Reprints: 24 free; charge for additional depends on article
length.

118 SOCIOLOGY OF EDUCATION

John I. Kitsuse, Department of Sociology, Northwestern University, Evanston, IL 60201
Publisher & Copyright: American Sociological Association,
1722 N. Street N.W., Washington, D.C. 20036
Subscriptions: Instit. $14/yr. Indiv. $10/yr. Available
on calendar-year basis only. Quarterly.

Description: "To provide a forum for studies of education by

scholars in all the social sciences from all‹parts of the
world. "
Typical Disciplines: Interdisciplinary--anthropology, economics, history, political science, psychology, sociology.
Special Features: Research reports; book reviews; research
notes; abstract for each article; advertising.

Acceptance/Rejection Procedures: Editorial board is interdisciplinary and international. MSS evaluated by colleagues in own field as well as other social scientists
to insure value and comprehensibility for whole audience.
Style Requirements: Consult journal; lines should be double
spaced and not longer than 6 inches; 3 copies of MS;
abstract of not more than 100 words required; enclose
stamped, return envelope; for anonymity, attach a cover
page giving authorship and institutional affiliation, but
provide only the title as a means of identification on the
MS itself.

119 TEACHERS COLLEGE RECORD (1900)
formerly, The Record

Frank G. Jennings, Teachers College, Columbia University,
525 W. 120th St., New York, N.Y. 10027
Publisher & Copyright: Teachers College, Columbia University
Subscriptions: Instit. & Indiv. $12/yr. Subscriptions begin
with Sept. or Feb. issue only. Quarterly. Ca. 6000.
150 pages/issue.

Description: "Is committed to bringing the latest thought in
education to the attention of its readers. It focuses its
editorial content both on the philosophical and practical
aspects of education and allied fields. "
Article Content: Education and psychology--both theoretical
and applied.
Intended Audience: Teachers; researchers; administrators;
practitioners; students.
Special Features: Research reports; theoretical articles;
book reviews; editorials; annual index; available on microform; advertising.

Acceptance/Rejection Criteria: MSS must be timely and directly related to education.
Acceptance/Rejection Procedures: MSS read by several reviewers.

Manuscript Disposition: Receipt of MS acknowledged; 6 weeks
   required for decision; rejected MS returned (enclose self-
   addressed stamped envelope); 20% submitted MSS accepted; 40 MSS published/yr.; 9 months from acceptance
   to publication.
Style Requirements: Consult journal; preferred length 3500
   to 5000 words, but flexible; 2 copies of MS; no abstract.
Payment: None to or by author.
Reprints: 50 without charge; charge for additional depends
   on length & amount ordered.

120   TODAY'S EDUCATION (1913) Journal of the National
      Education Association
      formerly, NEA Journal

Dr. Mildred S. Fenner, National Education Association, 1201
   16th St. N.W., Washington, D.C. 20036
Publisher & Copyright: National Education Association, 1201
   16th St. N.W., Washington, D.C. 20036
Subscriptions: Instit. & Indiv. $7/yr. Sent free to every
   NEA member. Quarterly. Ca. 1,500,000. 112 pages/
   issue.

Description: "The official quarterly magazine of the NEA.
   Its purpose is to keep educators informed about major
   developments in education. "
Intended Audience: Teachers and administrators at all levels;
   undergraduate and graduate students in education.
Special Features: Research reports; theoretical articles;
   book reviews; letters to the editor; editorials; hortatory
   or polemical articles; literature reviews, annual index,
   publication available on microform; advertising.

Acceptance/Rejection Criteria: Importance of educational
   topic; authority and reliability of MS; readability of MS;
   relevance.
Acceptance/Rejection Procedures: Most MSS are solicited.
   All unsolicited MSS are read carefully by several editors
   and an expert in the area covered. Decision is then
   made by the editor, and rejected MSS are returned with
   letters.
Manuscript Disposition: Receipt of MS acknowledged; 2
   months required for decision; rejected MS returned; 2%
   submitted MSS accepted; 100 MSS published/yr.
Style Requirements: NEA Style Book; preferred length of
   MS 800 to 4500 words, with 800 minimum and 4500

maximum length; one copy of MS; no abstract.
Payment: None to or by author.

121 URBAN EDUCATION (1966)

Warren Button, Faculty of Educational Studies, State Univer-
sity of New York at Buffalo, Buffalo, NY 14214
Publisher & Copyright: Sage Publications, Inc., 275 So.
Beverly Drive, Beverly Hills, CA 90212
Subscriptions: Instit. $15/yr. Indiv. $10/yr. Student $8/
yr. Quarterly. 128 pages/issue.

Description: "Exists to improve the quality of education in
the city by making the results of relevant empirical and
scholarly inquiry more generally available."
Article Content: Measurement and evaluation of pupil learning; assessment of the myriad intervening variables between intent and effect (for instance, of administrative
organization, of expenditures, or relationships with community and clientele, and of unanticipated results).
Typical Disciplines: Education; invites contributions from
other relevant fields such as jurisprudence, psychology,
sociology, political science, anthropology, economics,
philosophy, medicine, administration, and history.
Intended Audience: Teachers; researchers; administrators;
practitioners; students.
Special Features: Research reports; theoretical articles;
book reviews; literature reviews; special theme for some
issues; annual index; advertising.

Acceptance/Rejection Procedures: Each appropriate MS is
sent to 2 members of the journal's editorial advisory
board; these judgments are pooled and are used by the
editor in making final decisions; special issues are occasionally produced by guest editor(s), who solicits MSS.
Manuscript Disposition: Receipt of MS acknowledged; 7-11
weeks from receipt to decision; "blind" refereeing; rejected MS returned; 20-25% submitted MSS accepted; 35-
45 MSS published/yr.; 6-9 months from acceptance to
publication; generally first accepted, first published.
Style Requirements: Available upon request from editor or
publisher; preferred length 15-20 pages, double spaced;
2 copies of MS; no abstract.
Payment: None to or by author.
Reprints: 24 free; charge for additional depends on length.

122 VOCATIONAL GUIDANCE QUARTERLY (1952)

Daniel Sinick, George Washington University, Washington,
D.C. 20006
Publisher & Copyright: National Vocational Guidance Asso-
ciation.
Subscriptions: Instit. & Indiv. $8/yr. Membership in Na-
tional Vocational Guidance Association includes journal.
Subscriptions available from American Personnel &
Guidance Association, 1607 New Hampshire Ave. N.W.,
Washington, D.C. 20009. Quarterly. Ca. 15,000.
80 pages/issue.

Description: "Is the official publication of the National Vocational Guidance Association, a division of the American Personnel and Guidance Association. It is a professional journal basically concerned with the role of work
in the life of man (man, of course, embraces woman)."
Article Content: Vocational development; vocational planning;
occupational choice; preparation for occupations; labor
market dynamics; job finding; and job satisfaction.
Intended Audience: Counselors; guidance workers; personnel
workers; teachers; researchers; administrators; students.
Special Features: Research reports; theoretical articles;
letters to the editor; editorials; abstract for each article;
annual index; reports of programs and practices in "Practically Speaking" department; advertising.

Acceptance/Rejection Criteria: "Work" and "life" are interpreted broadly. The entire life span from earliest childhood to the retirement years may yield suitable topics
for presentation. Most useful if topic presented with implications for practice. Reports of research and discussions of theory are welcome, but authors are expected
to extend their conclusions to the realm of practical application. MSS must be prepared carefully with respect
to content and style. Logical organization is essential;
headings help to structure the content. Essential, too,
are clarity, accuracy, and conciseness.
Acceptance/Rejection Procedures: MSS ordinarily reviewed
by editorial board members.
Manuscript Disposition: Receipt of MS acknowledged; 2-3
months required for decision; rejected MS returned; critique to author; 20-25% submitted MSS accepted; 40 MSS
published/yr.; 6-9 months from acceptance to publication.
Style Requirements: Consult journal; preferred length 8 pages,

double spaced, or 2000 words; maximum length 12 pages or 3000 words; one-inch margin all around; original and 2 copies of MS; article titles and headings within article should be as short as possible; provide, but don't count, a cover page with author's name, position, and place of employment, and a succinct sentence (up to 30 words) summarizing the MS; reference style that of the Quarterly; avoid footnotes; use tables sparingly and type them on separate pages; reports for "Practically Speaking" should not exceed six typed double-spaced pages.

Payment: None to or by author.

Reprints: Senior author receives 10 copies of the journal; other contributors receive 5 copies.

STYLE MANUALS

Style manuals cited in the Subject Index are listed with either an address where the manual may be obtained or bibliographical information.

APA Publication Manual [style manual]. American Psychological Association; 1200 Seventeenth Street, N. W.; Washington, D. C. 20036

Campbell, William G. Form and Style in Thesis Writing. 3d ed. Boston: Houghton-Mifflin Company, 1969.

MLA Style Sheet. 2d ed. New York: Modern Language Association, 1972.

NEA Stylebook. National Education Association; 1201 Sixteenth Street, N. W.; Washington, D. C. 20036

Turabian, Kate L. A Manual for Writers of Term Papers, Theses, and Dissertations. 4th ed. Chicago: The University of Chicago Press, 1973.

University of Chicago Press Staff. A Manual of Style. 12th ed. Chicago: The University of Chicago Press, 1969.

INDICES AND ABSTRACTS

Abstracts for Social Workers. New York, New York, National Association of Social Workers. Quarterly.

Biological Abstracts. Philadelphia, Pennsylvania, BioSciences Information Service of Biological Abstracts. Semimonthly.

Canadian Education Index. Toronto, Canadian Education Association. Quarterly.

Child Development Abstracts and Bibliography. (Society for Research in Child Development). Chicago, Illinois, University of Chicago Press. 3 times/yr.

College Student Personnel Abstracts. Claremont, California. Claremont Institute for Administrative Studies, Claremont Graduate School. Quarterly.

Current Contents (Social, Behavioral Sciences) CC-SBS. Philadelphia, Pennsylvania, Institute for Scientific Information. Weekly.

Current Index to Journals in Education. (U.S. Office of Education; Educational Resources Information Center-- ERIC). New York, Macmillan Information Division, Macmillan Publishing Company. Monthly.

DSH Abstracts. Washington, D.C., Gallaudet College, Deafness, Speech and Hearing Publication. Quarterly.

Education Index. New York, H. W. Wilson Company. Monthly.

Educational Administration Abstracts. Columbus, Ohio. University Council for Educational Administration. 3 times/yr.

Exceptional Child Education Abstracts. Arlington, Virginia,
    The Council for Exceptional Children. Quarterly.

Excerpta Medica. Amsterdam, Netherlands, Excerpta Medica
    Foundation. (U.S. subscription address Nassau Bldg.,
    228 Alexander St., Princeton, New Jersey 08540.)

Index Medicus. Bethesda, Md., National Library of Medicine.
    Monthly.

LLBA--Language and Language Behavior Abstracts. Ann
    Arbor, Michigan, University of Michigan. Quarterly.

Psychological Abstracts. Washington, D.C., American Psy-
    chological Association. Monthly.

Poverty and Human Resources Abstracts. Ann Arbor, Michi-
    gan. Bimonthly.

Sage Urban Studies Abstracts. Beverly Hills, California,
    Sage Publications, Inc. Quarterly.

Sociological Abstracts. Editor Leo P. Chall, 73 8th Ave.,
    Brooklyn, New York 11215

Sociology of Education Abstracts. Editor D. F. Swift, In-
    formation for Education Ltd., 19 Abercromby Square,
    Liverpool L69 3BX, England, and Maxwell House,
    Elmsford, New York. Quarterly.

SUBJECT INDEX

Numerical citations are to serial numbers of title entries (not to page numbers). The citations reflect the principal content of the various journals as described in the 122 entries. Other journals may occasionally include the same content.

Accountability 28
Achievement testing 97
    see also Tests; Testing
Adjustment 70
Administration 26, 37, 42, 101, 115
Administrative behavior 37, 79
Admissions, college and university 23, 62, 115
Age and development 33
Aging 3
Alternative education 100
Altruistic compliance 114
Alumni assessment 115
Anthropology in education 100
Artificial intelligence 21
Arts 9
Assessment
    of alumni 115
    educational 12
    and evaluation 112
    personality 63, 86
    see also Evaluation; Measurement; Tests
Attitude
    change 60, 75, 87
    measurement 97
    research 114
Attitudes 60, 65

of citizens 36
of college students 22
Attribution 114, 115
Attribution processes 75
Authenticity 81

Bargaining 60
Behavior
    abnormal 56
        see also Psychopathology; Psychology, clinical
    administrative 37, 79
    and development 98
    dynamics 85
    economic-choice 83
    experimental analysis of 27, 57, 72
    human experience and 88
    modification 11, 30, 57, 60, 63
    motor 84
    pathological 56
    physical environment and 47
    sexual 10
    social 10, 65
Behavior research, mathematics and methodology of 73

137